D1431334

The

USES

of

DARKNESS

The
USES
of
DARKNESS

Women's Underworld Journeys,
Ancient and Modern

LAURIE BRANDS GAGNÉ

UNIVERSITY OF NOTRE DAME PRESS

Notre Dame, Indiana

Copyright 2000 by
University of Notre Dame Press
Notre Dame, Indiana 46556
All Rights Reserved
http://www.undpress.nd.edu

Manufactured in the United States of America

Library of Congress Cataloging-in-Publication Data
Gagné, Laurie Brands, 1951–
    The uses of darkness : women's underworld journeys,
    ancient, and modern / Laurie Brands Gagné.
        p.   cm.
    Includes bibliographical references and index.
        ISBN 0-268-04305-1 (alk. paper) — ISBN 0-268-04306-X
    (pbk. : alk. paper)
        1. Feminist theology.   2. Christian women—Religious
    life.   I. Title.
        BT83.55 .G34 2000
        230'.082—dc21
                                    00-009069

To all my students in "Women's Journey"
at Trinity College of Vermont,
whose honesty, enthusiasm, and willingness
to share their underworld journeys
have been an immense encouragement
to my writing of this book.

Contents

Preface

Jung has taught us that the soul expresses itself in a universal language of symbols. What we think we know and feel, he maintains, can be at odds with what our dreams and our artistic creations reveal about ourselves. To be whole, we must claim the figures of our symbolic expressions and interpret their meaning for our lives.

The first time I read the Sumerian story of the descent of the goddess Inanna into the underworld, I felt a shiver of recognition. In the figure of Ereshkigal, awesome hag-queen of the underworld, I encountered the form of my own buried rage. Though my upbringing was Catholic, in the symbol-system I had acquired, it seemed the central figure was a remote sky-god. The hag archetype was not included—except as something evil. The pre-Christian story allowed me to feel what I hadn't known I was feeling.

Discovering my soul's resonance with stories from the goddess tradition, which has its roots in our prehistoric ancestors' worship of the divine as feminine, gave me the idea that I could come to know myself—my buried self—by exploring that tradition. My initial conception of the book was a simple comparison between ancient stories portraying certain archetypal figures in a woman's psyche—not only the hag, but also the mother and the child—and their modern-day parallels. In Sylvia Plath's poetic persona, I could see the figure of Inanna. Novels by Joan Didion, Mary Gordon, and Virginia Woolf, like the Demeter-Persephone myth, all highlight the interplay of the mother-figure and the child-figure. Etty Hillesum's account of her spiritual journey—with its impetus in her soulful attraction to another—makes her a modern-day divine child or Psyche.

In writing the book, I soon realized that my interpretation of these ancient and modern stories was influenced by my own story, my own personal myth. My own story was one of love and loss. I never tell that story in the book, but, as subtext, it gives coherence to my treatment of the stories I tell—or re-tell. The underworld journey or experience of death that every story portrays I relate to as an experience of loss and in every case I am asking, "How does one come through loss?" Asking this question enabled me to see how the Inanna-Demeter-Psyche sequence of stories forms a progression: Inanna's rage only scratches the surface of what a woman is capable of in relating to loss and death; Demeter's acceptance and Psyche's trusting self-surrender disclose real spiritual depth.

When I turned to an investigation of the modern stories, I had to confront my residual fear of the sky-god of my childhood. Modern women seem to have further to go in integrating loss and death than their ancient counterparts. The self of many modern women has been damaged by the shame and guilt engendered by the image of God as stern Father or Judge. When someone like Sylvia Plath experiences loss, her overwhelming feeling is one of unworthiness, of failure. Modern women get stuck in the underworld, I found, when their incipient sense of inadequacy becomes active self-hatred. This tendency is expressed, archetypally, by the killing of the child. Only by turning to confront the mystery that the image of God as Judge obscures can a woman raised in a patriarchal religious tradition acquire a sense of self strong enough to integrate loss. The image from the goddess tradition of a woman giving birth to her divine child can brace a woman for this ordeal.

What is illustrated so beautifully by Etty Hillesum's story is the way that being in touch with your divine child—with your connection to the Living God—makes real, i.e., transcendent love possible. Etty notes that before she had a relationship with God, the passion she sometimes felt for others was "a desperate clinging." The knowledge of ourselves as related to God, she found, makes us capable of a pure passion. When someone is capable of a pure passion is when she can see how love and loss, love and death go together. This is the central insight of the ancient story of Eros and Psyche. When Etty enacts it, by letting go of the man she loves just because her love for him is transcendent and points beyond him to a life in love with God, she thinks she is doing something Christian. Working with Etty confirmed my belief that drawing on the wisdom of the goddess tradition can help modern men and women make a meaningful re-appropriation of Christianity.

Much work has been done by Christian feminists in recent years to free the Christian tradition and theology from patriarchal distortions.[1] I think of my work as contributing to that effort. But whereas the usual approach for a feminist theologian is simply to critique these distortions from a more authentic spiritual standpoint, I have tried to retrace the steps by which a person might come to attain such a standpoint. One's spiritual journey can only begin with the experience of the Holy, the conception of God one has. If that conception is idolatrous, it can be left behind only by personal spiritual growth; rational argument is little help. My approach demonstrates the religious significance not just of the higher standpoint but of every groping gesture in its direction.

On a more universal plane, this book speaks, I believe, to the primitive religiosity of many people today. Modern intellectual culture, perhaps, is secular, but popular culture (which, especially in America, affects all of us more than we might care to admit) is riven with the kind of longings that, on examination, prove to be religious. The longing I zero in on is the desire for a true love—that "ancient fairy tale,"[2] as Virginia Woolf calls it, that inspires young people to dream and makes their elders dissatisfied. However sturdy the fabric of our lives in terms of work and relationships, the heart's longing for someone or something worthy of devotion creates a rent in the fabric. The image of a true love that most people have, at least initially, is too dependent on sensible beauty to qualify as an image of God and hence, their desire is more erotic than spiritual; this is what makes us primitives. Yet if we are willing to go to the root of our longing,[3] as Carol Flinders puts it, we find that its origin is deeper than erotic desire. If we persist in the task of coming to know ourselves, coming to know our hearts, our longing becomes manifest as a truly transcendent orientation. The women's stories I explicate represent stepping stones on the path to this discovery.

The book is structured similarly to a course, "The Woman's Journey, Ancient and Modern," which I have been teaching at Trinity College of Vermont for the past twelve years. Though the vast majority of students in the course have been women, the occasional male student has professed to find the course material relevant to his life experience. One of them said, "This isn't the woman's journey; it's the human journey—from a woman's point of view." On the other hand, I recently gave a talk on the material presented in chapter four and one of the men in the audience commented, "This is exactly the kind of thing that men today need to hear, but are unwilling to hear." I didn't write this book for women; I wrote it for myself. It stands to reason that anyone who has experienced love and loss and struggled with loss; anyone whose spirit has been suppressed by an overbearing Father/God but will not, for all that, reject Christianity, may find some benefit in it.

It was my teacher at Notre Dame, the theologian John Dunne, who showed me how exciting theology can be when its starting point is the individual's life story. Everyone familiar with his spiritual vision will see that I am indebted to him for certain key ideas, the most fundamental being that of the spiritual journey. It was reading Simone Weil, though, and also Kierkegaard, that convinced me not to reject the Christian point of view just because my native experience of God was so painful. To the students in "Woman's Journey" who have shared their struggles over the years, I am deeply grateful. We have cried, but we have also laughed together and the depth of our laughter would not have been possible, we realized, without the tears.

The Alternative Tradition

DARK LOVE AND PURE LOVE

When one is bursting with sensuality—whether as a young person becoming acquainted with the delicious sensations of the body for the first time or as a mature person exploring the depths of sexual passion—the life of the spirit can seem alien. What is more compelling, at first blush, than beauty that is tangible—that can be held and stroked and possessed? And what can root itself more firmly in the soul than the image of someone we desire? St. Augustine, a highly sensual individual, acknowledges the importance of sensuality to the whole person when he declares that the Word of God was revealed in the flesh so that "what was visible to the heart alone could become visible also to the eye and so heal men's hearts."[1] St. Augustine was speaking of Jesus, of course, and of how Jesus visible to the eye could "heal men's hearts," but he is also saying something about the interconnection of body and soul, flesh and spirit. His statement implies that our sensuality is at the very heart of ourselves—and thus, to deny it is to deny something essential to the persons that we are. The power of sensuality, then, ultimately derives from the heart. It is the heart's response to beauty. If we could conceive of the life of the spirit as a journey of the heart, it would not seem foreign to our sensuality. Indeed, the awakening of one's sensuality might appear as the beginning of one's spiritual journey.

What stands in the way of thinking of the life of spirit as a journey of the heart is a long tradition of spiritual masters, beginning with Plato, who emphasize the mind's role in our pursuit of the Good. The desire to soar above material reality to attain a kind of pinnacle of human experience is what prompts this version of the quest. In St. Bonaventure's *Mind's Journey to God*, one proceeds by a process of abstraction from earthly things: from finding traces of God in the workings of one's own mind to the ultimate contemplation of God as Being-Itself.[2] To be sure, the heart is not absent from this process. Bonaventure says, "one is not disposed to contemplation which leads to mental elevation unless one be with Daniel a man of desires."[3] But Bonaventure distinguishes between two ways in which desires are enkindled in us: "by the cry of prayer, which makes one groan with the murmuring of one's heart, and by a flash of apprehension by which the mind turns most directly and intensely to the rays of light."[4] Though he invites the reader to the cry of prayer in the prologue to his work, it is the mind's "flash of apprehension" which leads from one stage to the next on the journey he describes.

There is something analogous to the "cry of prayer," which Bonaventure commends as a way of enkindling desires, in the awakening of one's sensuality. Bonaventure is referring to prayer that is directed at Jesus, but one can also cry out in a kind of prayer "that makes one groan with the murmuring of one's heart" in invoking the beautiful person that one desires. One thinks of Rogozhin, in *The Idiot*, becoming "all aflame in an instant" on seeing Nastasya Filippovna for the first time, and of the way he lies awake all that night thinking of her.[5] Rogozhin's passion, of course, is ultimately destructive, for the book ends with his murder of Nastasya, but in his passion, we get a glimpse of the great man he could have been. Not everyone, it seems, is capable of passion, of becoming "all aflame in an instant." Most people live with guarded hearts, fearful of losing control of themselves, of acting crazy or foolish. Rogozhin, however, is vulnerable. His all-consuming passion is a dark form, as it were, of the mystic's love of God. But how does one move from a passion that is dark and full of tragic potential to a pure passion? From the standpoint of dark passion a passion that is pure seems impossible. "If it is pure, it is not passion," one is tempted to think, "but rather, an abstract way of being in relationship."

Can the love of God really be a passion? If I think of the religious people with whom I am familiar, the answer seems to be no. "Love is not emotion," I hear them say, and I find myself wondering what love is for them. I think of Lady Marchmain, in Evelyn Waugh's *Brideshead Revisited,* whom her daughter Cordelia describes, after her death, as "not a saint, but saintly," implying that her mother had the appearance of sainthood, but not its substance.[6] The striking feature of Lady Marchmain is that she is incapable of intimacy. She seems to love an abstract ideal of the people around her—her children, her admirers—rather than the people themselves. When she loses someone she loves, whether it be her husband to another woman or her son to alcohol, she is more disappointed in them, for having failed her, than bereft. We can imagine that her prayers are directed, as well, to a God she approves of, rather than the Living God. In contrast to Lady Marchmain, we have this from Catherine of Siena, a bona fide saint:

> . . . O immeasurably tender love! Who would not be set afire with such love? What heart could keep from breaking? You, deep well of charity, it seems that you are so madly in love with your creatures that you could not live without us. Yet you are our God, and have no need of us. Your greatness is no greater for our well-being, nor are you harmed by any harm that comes to us, for you are supreme eternal Goodness. What could move you to such mercy? Neither

duty nor any need you have of us . . . but only love! . . . My
heart is breaking and yet cannot break for the hungry longing it has conceived for you.[7]

From Rogozhin's dark passion to Catherine's "hungry
longing" is a journey. It is the kind of journey one may begin
without realizing it—which makes it very different from
Bonaventure's explicit "assault on the heavens." Like Charles,
the main character of Brideshead Revisited, one may simply feel,
in falling in love, that one has discovered a wonderful secret,
the "key to the door of an enchanted garden," and instead of
seeing this experience as pointing beyond itself, one may try to
stay in the "enchanted garden."[8] Charles acts blindly in his
loves—going from his youthful idyll with Sebastian to his mature passion for Julia, to what he calls his "love affair with the
army," all unthinking—until, middle-aged and loveless, he
finds himself back at Brideshead unlocking the door of his
memories. First, the image of Sebastian and then, Julia, beautiful Julia, take form and rend his heart as he tells the story of his
time with them. Finally, when he has told the story through to
the end, he enters the chapel at Brideshead. In the darkness,
he seems to discover, as symbolized by the burning sanctuary
lamp, the pure flame of the love of God in his heart. It is only
then that he sees his past loves as prelude—as a kind of prepa-
ration for the love new born in him:

> Something quite remote from anything the builders in-
> tended has come out of their work and out of the fierce little
> human tragedy in which I played, something none of us
> thought about at the time: a small, red flame . . . it could
> not have been lit but for the builders and the tragedians.[9]

Telling the story of his lost loves is the key to Charles's
discovery of a new love, a pure love, that can glow in his heart
and light his way even when, as he says, he is "homeless, child-
less, middle-aged, and loveless."[10] Telling the story of one's past
is a way of releasing oneself from the thrall of old loves, lost

loves. It is when we are enthralled by passion that it is dark, so that what appears to be an "enchanted garden" is potential for a "fierce little human tragedy." But if we tell the story of our past loves through to the end, the way Charles does when he recounts his parting with Julia and the avalanche it was in his life, we find ourselves at a different standpoint than when we began. All that time, we can imagine, her image locked in his heart held him in thrall. Telling the story releases the image and frees up his heart so that when he walks into the chapel he is open to the new love he discovers there. The bridge from dark love to pure love, it seems, is the story that frees the heart of its enthralling images.

There is a tradition in Western literature of stories that free the heart of dark love. It is the tradition of women's stories of the underworld. The underworld journey, as women portray it, is basically an experience of the dark side of passion, of the rage and wretchedness which accompany the frustration of desire. In recounting underworld journeys, what is effected, first of all, is a catharsis of one's rage and wretchedness. This is probably the primary contribution of this tradition. But some stories of the underworld portray creative ways of relating to it. They present women returning from the underworld, having made a wonderful discovery. These stories of the underworld imply that dark love can be redeemed—that love that is blind and potentially destructive can flower into the pure love that Charles experiences.

A SPIRITUAL PROGRESSION

It may seem strange to identify the experience that gives rise to women's stories of the underworld as an experience of the "dark side of passion." Underworld journeys are always presented as visits to the land of the dead. To find oneself in the underworld is to be exiled from the land of the living and under the sway of the god or goddess of the dead. It would seem to be an experience of the power of death rather than an experience of the power of passion that gives rise to stories of the underworld. But there is a connection between the power of passion and the power of death. It is a connection we recognize implicitly when we hesitate before surrendering ourselves to a passionate engagement with another. In that moment of hesitation, we seem to realize that in abandoning ourselves to passion, in letting it determine our life's course, we run the risk of losing that life should the one we love passionately withdraw from the relationship. The withdrawal of the other, in this case, is an experience of the power of death. It amounts to the end of the life one entered through relationship with the other. In the most ancient story of an underworld journey that we know of, the Sumerian story of the goddess Inanna's descent (*ca.* 2,000 B.C.E.), the connection between the power of passion and the power of death is conveyed by making the goddess of love and beauty, Inanna, the sister of Ereshkigal, the fearsome queen of the underworld.[11]

It is the connection between love and death that can make the truly passionate individual heroic. We normally think of heroes as doing great deeds—slaying monsters, for example, the way Gilgamesh, hero of Sumerian epic, slays Humbaba, the monster who guards the cedar forest.[12] But I would maintain that it is the element of risk involved in accomplishing the deed that essentially distinguishes the hero. Gilgamesh is risking his life in confronting Humbaba. Is it such a stretch of the imagination to envision the person who gives herself to a passionate love as a kind of Gilgamesh or Odysseus or Aeneas? To be sure, the life one risks losing in the surrender to passion is not the same as one's physical existence, which is what Gilgamesh risked. One continues to exist in the aftermath of a tragedy such as the loss of a great love. But we can rightly say, in such a case, that the life has gone out of one's existence, for life is more than mere existence. To be vitally alive, as we know whenever we say yes to a new opportunity and experience an upsurge of the life-force or desire to live in ourselves, we must have a strong will to live. Our physical existence is affected by the absence of the life-force. Someone who has lost the life he or she shared with another and not found a new life to replace it can be so lacking in the will to live that his or her physical existence is endangered.

Discovering a new life through the surrender to passion, losing that life through the loss of the other, and coming through loss—this is the basic pattern of experience that is the context of women's stories of the underworld. Some of the stories, like the Sumerian "Inanna's Descent," leave out the first two parts of this paradigm, focusing solely on the experience of coming through loss. That Inanna's story implies the prior experiences of love and loss is indicated, at the end of the story, when she chooses her partner Dumuzi as her replacement in the underworld. Once the object of her passion (as recounted in "The Courtship of Inanna and Dumuzi"[13]), he is now the victim of her wrath. The difference in the goddess's attitude toward Dumuzi between "The Courtship" and "The Descent" implies an experience of estrangement or loss. Other stories of the underworld telescope the scenes of love and loss. In the myth of Demeter and Persephone,[14] for example, Persephone's ecstasy in the sunlit meadow gives way, immediately, to her abduction by Hades. The moment of loss is almost simultaneous with the moment of love. Other stories of the underworld are tucked into love stories—as is the case with "Eros and Psyche."[15] Psyche's underworld journey is a brief, though crucial, section of the long myth which recounts her love and loss of Eros and the ordeals she undergoes to be reunited with him.

I am beginning my study of the passage from dark love to pure love, from a passion that is enthralling to one that is uplifting, by interpreting the three ancient myths just mentioned—"Inanna's Descent," the Demeter and Persephone myth, and "Eros and Psyche." From the Sumerian story of Inanna to the Homeric hymn to Demeter is about 1,200 years and from Demeter to Psyche, another 1,000 or so. As well as a chronological progression, these three myths represent a spiritual progression—a deepening of one's capacity to relate to one's life, in this case, to the loss of life we have been describing as the "dark side of passion." Inanna's underworld journey is portrayed as the ascendancy of the hag-queen over the goddess, indicating the takeover of the personality by the dark forces in the psyche. In the *Hymn to Demeter,* the victory of the dark forces is only partial: not the goddess herself, but her daughter is depicted as enslaved by the god of the underworld. Psyche's story represents a reversal of the other two in that instead of losing her beauty in the underworld, she returns from her journey with the treasure of divine beauty. From Inanna's enthrallment by dark forces, to Demeter's active relationship with them, to Psyche's experience of redemption of the dark side of her personality—these stories reflect an unfolding or emergence of the human spirit.

In relating these myths to each other, instead of to their ritual contexts, I am departing from the trend of contemporary scholarship. Many scholars today, in studying ancient texts, especially those portraying goddess figures, are seeking an alternative to the Judeo-Christian tradition of worshiping God the Father. Consequently, they use these texts as a way of "getting back" to the religion of the Goddess, which dominated the culture of Europe and the Near East throughout the Neolithic period and Copper Age (7,000–3,500 B.C.E.) and probably typified the religious outlook of human beings in these areas as early as 100,000 B.C.E.[16] Representation of the Goddess took many forms: stone figurines with pronounced breasts and buttocks, womb-like cave sanctuaries, hybrid representations that are part female figure and part bird or snake, androgynous figures with phallus-shaped heads, and a variety of animal figures representing the Goddess's double—the butterfly, the pig, the owl.[17] From the artifacts of Goddess religion, which are all we have to go on since there are no texts from this period, it seems that the Goddess stood for nature as an interplay of powers, especially the powers of life and death.

Nature was understood as feminine because, in prehistoric times, human beings were particularly in awe of the life-giving power of women's bodies. To be born, for them, was to be released, not only from your mother's womb, but from the great womb of nature; to die was to return to it. Compared to the Goddess, who combines in herself all the powers of the natural world, the goddesses of historic times seem diminished. This is the view, at any rate, of such authors as Charlene Spretnak and Carol Christ. In discussing the Greek goddesses, Spretnak differentiates the Olympians of the classical period portrayed by Homer from the "pre-Hellenic goddesses" known through artifacts, the oral tradition, and passing references in classical sources to very old observances of Goddess religion still taking place at certain sites in Greece.[18] Spretnak describes the earlier goddesses as "wise, powerful" and "autonomous," in contrast to the later female deities who are "petty, jealous" and "victimized."[19] As a feminist, she sees this relative devaluation of the feminine in classical Greek religion as a result of the cultural shift from matriarchal (female-centered) to patriarchal (male-centered) institutions and consciousness accomplished through the Ionian, Achaean, and Dorian invasions (2,500–1,000 B.C.E.). The invaders introduced, she says, deities who were warlike, judgmental, and remote from human beings so that the religious focus shifted "upward," away from the "energy forces" experienced in everyday life that were celebrated by Goddess religion.[20] Both she and Carol Christ believe that the empowerment of modern women, religiously, requires stepping back through the existing texts to the point where the Goddess, unencumbered by patriarchy, reigned supreme in human minds. In her book, *The Laughter of Aphrodite,* Christ recounts her own participation in Goddess rituals—and the numinous experiences they engendered—which highlighted pilgrimages she made to ancient sites of Goddess worship.[21]

There is no question that the Goddess of the Neolithic period—and the pre-patriarchal goddesses who succeeded her—were more powerful figures than the heroines of the three ancient myths under discussion. Though hailed as "queen of heaven and earth," the goddess Inanna was a subordinate member of the Sumerian pantheon. In the story "The Huluppu Tree," Inanna, as a maiden goddess, is described as walking "in fear of the word of" her great-grandfather "the Sky God An" and "in fear of the word of" her grandfather "the Air God Enlil."[22] As a mature goddess, she is capable of matching wits with her male superiors—as when she tricks Enki, the god of wisdom, into giving her all the *me*, the "holy laws of heaven and earth," in his possession.[23] But because of her relative insignificance, the mortal Gilgamesh feels free not only to reject her advances when she tries to seduce him after his conquest of Humbaba, but to heap insults on her as well.[24] Unlike the great Goddess, who personified the totality of all the powers, Inanna's power has been restricted to that of sexuality or, more broadly construed, fertility—the generative power of human beings, plants, and animals. As an earth goddess, Demeter enjoyed a certain independence from the Greek gods and goddesses—Zeus foremost among them—who dwelt on Mount Olympus. She and Dionysius reigned over the rites of the harvest as a sphere separate from the various arenas of the Olympians. But more important than her role as a goddess of the grain was that of suffering mother. The Eleusinian mysteries, which re-enacted Demeter's anguished search for her daughter, far surpassed in sacred significance the harvest festivals we associate with her. Since Demeter's suffering was caused by none other than Zeus—who arranged, we are told, the marriage between her daughter and Hades—we must conclude that she, like Inanna, was a lesser member of the pantheon to which she belonged. Psyche, not a goddess, but a creature of unearthly beauty, is the most victimized of the three heroines. Her spiritual journey begins when she is chained to a crag at the top of a mountain and left to die—the measure taken by her father, the king, to appease the god's wrath.

However reduced in stature compared to the great Goddess and her prehistoric successors, Inanna, Demeter, and Psyche strike me as extremely important role models for women. I am suggesting that we read their stories not as religious texts to be used to evoke a numinous experience— whether of nature or of any of the powers in particular—but as religious texts in the sense of wisdom literature: guides for one's life journey. As stories, these texts are independent of their ritual contexts. We can derive insight from Inanna's struggle with the hag-queen, Demeter's struggle with Zeus, and Psyche's ordeals even if we know little about the Sumerian, Greek, and Hellenistic religious settings that are their historical points of origin. The psychological and spiritual realism of the texts make them universal. It is this realism which makes them more valuable, to me, than any numinous experience which might be engendered by "getting behind" them to prehistoric Goddess rituals. I am profoundly moved by those moments in which I discover—and re-discover—my inherent connection with nature and my capacity for an ecstatic participation in the "energy forces" to which Charlene Spretnak refers. Who is not drawn by the mysterious power of the ocean and re-vitalized by playing in the surf? Who does not feel a pang remembering certain moments of sexual ecstasy or the even deeper experiences of the life-force that accompany childbirth? My intention is not to minimize such experiences, nor the sense of awe and childlike wonder they re-awaken in us. Rather, I would point out that no experience of the life-force, however wonderful, solves the basic problem for human beings—which is what to do when it is not life but the power of death that we are experiencing. Surely, our prehistoric ancestors had a way of responding to the power of death. It was probably a bloodier, more violent way than current enthusiasts of Goddess worship envision. These enthusiasts, however much they acknowledge that the Goddess personified *both* the powers of life and the powers of death, tend to focus, almost exclusively, on her life-giving aspect and downplay the violence that must have been engendered by her dark side.[25] The great contribution of the Inanna, Demeter, and Psyche stories is that they equally confront the dark side of the powers, specifically, the dark side of passion.

If we want to avoid the utopian thinking characteristic of some feminists who call for a revival of Goddess religion in our time, we must be willing to face the whole truth about ourselves as human beings. There is a child in us capable of ecstasy, but there is also a monster who can be extremely brutal. Facing the power of death—as a gut-wrenching reality and not an abstract proposition—we become aware of the monster. We find ourselves turning cold and hard. It is not surprising that Charles Ryder joins the army after the loss of his life with Julia. Heroines who enact our relationship with the monster are more helpful, to me, than goddess figures reduced to their nurturing, life-giving aspects. Indeed, such figures turn out to be projections of what we want the divine to be, rather than expressions of an actual experience of the divine. A child playing ecstatically in the waves is having a one-sided experience of the divine unless that experience is tinged with dread. The real prehistoric Goddess, not the one in the minds of many contemporary feminists, must have evoked fear as well as love. The vultures on the walls of the temple at Catal Huyuk attacking decapitated human corpses, which scholars tell us are representations of the Goddess (ca. 6,500–5,000 B.C.E.) are certainly fearsome.[26] Indeed, the dreadful queen of the Sumerian underworld, Ereshkigal, appears to be their direct descendant. Facing the power of death—the destructive side of the divine—calls forth the best as well as the worst in a person. To know we are struggling with a monster, after all, represents an advance over not knowing and gives us an edge in the struggle.

In my interpretation of the Inanna, Demeter, and Psyche myths, I will be focusing on the change of heart that brings about a new awareness in each story. It is the progression, both in awareness and in the corresponding relationship with the dark side that they portray, which makes these writings representative of a spiritual journey. Demeter's story is not only different from Inanna's, it reflects a higher or deeper standpoint in experience than that of the Sumerian story. Psyche's myth, in turn, goes beyond the insights into the dark side that inspired *Hymn to Demeter*. By tracing a progression in the myths I interpret, I am implying a kind of evolution in the ability of human beings to relate to the dark side. In Hegelian fashion, I see this progression recapitulated in the life-stories of individuals in later periods who undertook this way of conversion and redemption. Thus, though the Inanna, Demeter, and Psyche myths are categorized, by theologians, as "pagan" literature, we will see their themes and insights recurring in the works of contemporary authors, to be discussed in later chapters, whose religious influence has been primarily Judeo-Christian. A Christian myself, I can feel the resonance of these ancient myths with my own life-story. The spiritual journey I intend to articulate is personal, for me, as well as universal.

THE ALTERNATIVE TRADITION

The stories we are about to study became important to me when I was trying to free myself of my own enthrallment by God the Father. Growing up female in a traditional Roman Catholic family, I pictured the divine as a Judge whose approval I could win by measuring up to certain very definite standards of perfection. These were, in large part, derived from the opinions of my biological father, whom I adored. My childhood was spent "being good," so as to win one of my father's rare words of praise, which meant, I believed, that God Himself was smiling on me. As a young woman, I fell in love with one father-figure after another until the moment when, defeated in my quest for perfection and filled with fear and trembling, I confronted God and found that the Living God is compassionate. That put the first chink in the armor that allegiance to the divine Judge had given me. I was to find, however, that it is one thing to experience a moment of release and another to enact that insight in one's life, day to day. Unless one's experience is captured in new images which make possible new ways of thinking about the divine, it is all too easy to fall back into old, constricting patterns of behavior. Afraid to name my experience with my own words and appropriate the freedom that it offered, I sought out other, traditional ways of imaging the divine and discovered the goddesses and the tradition of women's underworld journeys. My appreciation of this tradition represents my first break with patriarchal modes of religious expression.

In turning to the goddesses, however, I never thought of abandoning the Living God of my experience. Whatever difficulty I had translating the meaning of that sacred encounter into new ways of thinking and acting, my heart was forever changed by it and had formed a new allegiance. I guess I was looking for the reflection of equally transforming moments in the literature I investigated. It seemed to me that others surely knew the secret I had discovered, that knowledge of the Living God—who released one from the enthrallment of sheer power—was the basis of all true religion. Goddess mythology appealed to me because it seemed to represent the experience of the divine from a feminine point of view, the lack of which I had suffered, as a girl-child. I have since discovered, through my male students, that men are apt to relate just as readily to these texts as women. What that says to me is that the feminine religious perspective is felt as lacking in our culture, by *both* men and women. Men suffer the repressiveness of patriarchal structures, too. But as a woman, I felt that I had been severely damaged by my years in the service of a judgmental God the Father. I didn't know how to be a free woman, which meant that I didn't know how to be myself. The exigencies of that God had left me as stiff and unyielding as a statue. By studying the goddesses, I hoped to learn about myself—myself in relation to the Living God.

It may seem strange for a Christian woman to turn to the Goddess tradition—specifically, that tradition's account of underworld journeys—for ways to envision and relate to the Living God. Yet what I have come to understand is that every moment in which the heart is released and the mind illumined is an experience of God. The Living God was known, long before Christianity, whenever people opened their hearts to the dreadful mystery from which life and death ensue. Surely the Goddess was an image of that dreadful mystery for our prehistoric ancestors. If most of them lived in fear and fascination of the divine, the way I lived, for years, in the fear and fascination of God the Father, some of them must have made the breakthrough that I did: in an unguarded or desperate moment they must have come through the enthrallment of God's power to the open spaces of God's love. "Thou Living Dread, whose fountains yet flow mercy," Cain says, in the play *The Death of Eve* by William Vaughan Moody, which portrays Eve overcoming her fear and turning to face God at last.[27] We have no record of their prayers and invocations—only hints from documents that come to us from hundreds of years later— but why should we not think that men and women worshiping the Goddess addressed Her in similar terms? Fear of the Holy is endemic to all religions. When your back is to God and your heart protected, fear of the Holy can hold you in thrall. The turning is what is essential, for the Living God is revealed only to unprotected hearts. Our prehistoric ancestors, we must assume, found facing the Holy no more difficult—and no easier—than we do.

An adequate understanding of the Goddess tradition, it seems to me, must take into account both the moment of fear or dread one experiences in relating to the divine and the moment of breakthrough, in which one's dread is dissolved in the heart's release. In my experience, there is no heart's release without dread, which is to say that our hearts are not naturally open to the divine, that there is a prior stage when the heart's ignorance keeps us focused on power as the essential attribute of the being or beings we worship. "Every woman adores a Fascist."[28] This is Sylvia Plath's way of saying that what attracts us, first of all—when our hearts are still closed—is that sheen that magically attaches itself to possessors of force. The wonder is, I suppose, that we ever get beyond this primal attraction to discover the real essence of the divine. But this is where the underworld journey is so important. When it is the dark side of life that we are experiencing—when we are beset by illness, loss, betrayal, or any of the host of woes that is part of the human condition—through sheer desperation we are apt to overcome our fear of the divine. At this point, we may turn and even if we turn to cringe before God, it is enough. If we have really turned, sooner or later, we find ourselves standing upright. The heart's release is to know oneself, in Christian terms, as an "image of God," a being akin and not alien—*even in our weakness*—to the Being that we worship.

In Inanna's, Demeter's, and Psyche's journeys, we will find moments of dread and moments of breakthrough. If we come from the tradition of God the Father, however, we must expect to find these breakthroughs in unexpected places. In that tradition, epiphanies characteristically occur on the heights—think of Abraham on Mount Moriah, Moses on Mount Sinai, Elijah against all the prophets of Baal on Mount Carmel. This seems to suggest a sublime experience of the Living God, one that is mediated by spiritual ecstasy—an experience of soaring in which the line that separates the self from God disappears. The Hebrew prophets had this experience to such an extent that they used the first person in uttering the Lord's judgment on Israel.[29] In contrast, we think of "shady groves" when we think of epiphanies in the Goddess tradition. (Once I came to a large crucifix that had been placed in the very center of a shady grove and found myself wondering why a statue of Pan wasn't there instead.) "Shady groves" are symbolic of an earthier experience of the divine, one which is mediated aesthetically, especially through the beauty of nature. If it is the line between the self and the God-

beyond-the-world that disappears in religious ecstasy characteristic of the God-the-Father tradition, it is the line between
the self and the God-within-the-world that blurs when one is
caught up in the peak experiences of the Goddess tradition.
What one feels is oneness with the life-force that animates all
things. Susan Griffin writes,

> when I let this bird fly to her own purpose, when this bird
> flies in the path of his own will, the light from this bird en-
> ters my body, and when I see the beautiful arc of her flight, I
> love this bird, when I see the arc of her flight, I fly with her,
> enter her in my mind, leave myself, die for an instant, live
> in the body of this bird whom I cannot live without. . . .[30]

In Inanna's, Demeter's, and Psyche's stories, as a matter
of fact, shady groves are present but do not figure prominently.
In the courtship portion of Inanna's story, her love for Dumuzi
is portrayed as coming to a climax in the apple orchard where
she "pour[s] out plants from [her] womb" and "place[s] plants
before him" and "pour[s] out grain from [her] womb" and
"place[s] grain before him."[31] But her underworld journey, as
we would expect, contains no reference to a shady grove.
Demeter's story begins with her daughter playing in a sunlit
meadow—the place of her subsequent abduction by Hades—
but, after that, the story follows the mother's grim search for
her daughter and her wandering among the "cities of men"
until she withdraws into her temple. Psyche enjoys the longest
sojourn in a "shady grove," really a magical mountain valley
where her lover's castle is located, but the crucial part of her
journey begins when she leaves it. What is interesting is that
the ecstasy of "peak experiences" is not the focus of these stories. That suggests that the journey they portray is not primarily about self-transcendence. Instead, we could say, its goal
is self-transformation. More precisely, we could posit two
turning points of the journey: the moment of transcendence,
when the heroine is lifted out of herself by the power of passion, which quickly gives way in each story to the underworld

journey, and the moment of transformation, which brings the heroine in each case back from the underworld.

Transcendence followed by transformation—we seem to have come upon the formula for *all* spiritual journeys. A movement beyond the self, which gives one the sense of wonderful possibilities—indeed, the Kierkegaardian sense that "all things are possible"[32]—and a movement or change within the self that amounts to realizing a wonderful possibility. Transcendence without transformation would be incomplete. It is natural to "come down" from a peak experience and ask, "But what was it *for?* What does it mean for my life?" To enjoy moments of transcendence without being open to transformation would be to abort a natural process. In the God-the-Father tradition there are numerous examples of transcendence followed by transformation—the most striking, perhaps, being found in the Exodus story. The exaltation of the Israelites' deliverance from Egypt followed by the dramatic appearance of Yahweh on Mount Sinai gives way, very quickly, to their forty years of wandering in the wilderness. As difficult as it was, the Israelite prophets looked back on the wilderness experience as a positive time in Israel's history. They saw it as a kind of crucible in which the Israelites were transformed into the people of Yahweh.[33] We should look on the dark experience of the underworld in the Goddess tradition as a kind of crucible as well. After the moment of exaltation, when one is lifted out of oneself by the power of passion, comes the time of darkness in which one begins to be capable of a passionate existence.

This is the possibility that the Goddess tradition seems to hold up as realizable: a passionate existence, being heart-and-soul engaged in one's life. In an ecstatic response to a beautiful person we glimpse precisely this possibility. How wonderful to feel this way, we think. How wonderful it would be to feel this way all the time. The desire to possess the other person which usually follows the initial ecstasy is an expression, it seems, of the longing for a permanent passion, for one's life to be given over to the person or thing that one loves passionately. The question arises, why is the loss of the other necessary to the realization of a passionate existence? Why can't we simply enjoy perpetual bliss with the other? The answer is that however marvelous the ecstasy, however prolonged that experience of crossing the line that separates me from the other, me from the world, I always come back to myself. I come back unwillingly, but I come back. It is unavoidable. And in the lucid moment that follows ecstasy, I realize that I am *not* a passionate person. Passion can course through me like a river of light, but its source is beyond me. When it ebbs, there is nothing I can do to renew the flow. To become capable of a passionate *existence*, I must be transformed.

Is it really possible to be "heart and soul engaged in one's life" or permanently open to the source of that power that courses through one, on occasion, in the ecstatic response to beauty? Do we want too much in wanting that, in imagining that? If it were simply the *experience* that we were after, then the answer would be Yes, it *is* asking too much to be perpetually ecstatic, for even in the most passionate engagement with another, we always come back to ourselves. What *is* it that we want, then, if a continual ecstatic experience is impossible? What is possible, it seems, is receptivity—or openness, as we have been calling it—to the source of passion, rather than simply to the experience of passion. What a difference there is between these two standpoints! Openness to passion as an experience, especially if it takes precedence in one's life, might lead to a preoccupation with magic—an attempt to control the various powers that we associate with passion. Openness to the source of passion, on the other hand, would amount to nothing less than a relationship with the Living God—the source of all the powers in the universe.

In the Goddess tradition, transcendence followed by transformation turns out to mean the development of the capacity for relationship—relationship, first of all, with the Living God, but, as a corollary, relationship also with all living things. From that first experience of beauty that pierces the heart, there is a progression to being heart-open to the beauty that is in everything. The constant, in this tradition, it turns out, is beauty. First we love the beauty that is tangible—"that can be held and stroked and possessed." Then we suffer the loss of the beauty that we love. But if we persevere in our love—through the darkness of loss or estrangement—we become capable, the Goddess tradition seems to promise, of perceiving and loving beauty that is intangible—that lies at the heart of every creature. The Living God, in the Goddess tradition, is not beyond the world, but at its inmost center. Understood this way, the Goddess tradition does not seem so far removed from that of God the Father, with its doctrine of the *Logos* or the presence of the Word of God in all that is. Yet, in my opinion, this doctrine, with its implications for our view of the world—both the natural world and the world created by humans—has been neglected. The image of God the Father—all powerful, all seeing, all just—has overshadowed it. Perhaps through the door of the Goddess tradition, Christians can rediscover its import.

What I am attempting in my study of women's journeys through the underworld is to reclaim the wisdom contained in these stories for heirs of the God-the-Father tradition. The alternative tradition these journeys represent has much to offer us. It is with great sorrow that I reflect on the damage that the idol of God the Father has done over the centuries. Largely because of it, we are a civilization that is cut off from the natural world and from that precious part of ourselves that is earthy and sensual. We fear beauty and in its place have put the sterile products of our frenzy to accomplish something. But the void of beauty in our lives cannot be ignored. Is not the gratuitous violence of our time symptomatic of this great ache in our souls? Does not our inability to sustain relationships indicate that we are too willing to harden ourselves to the beauty of the other? Beauty is all around us, but it is the rare person who perceives it acutely. Only if we expose ourselves to it can the journey to a passionate existence begin. To be sure, there are many places in the God-the-Father tradition where beauty is acknowledged as a reflection of God's glory—the hint that God is supreme Beauty: "The heavens declare the glory of God / And the firmament proclaims his handiwork" (Psalm 19). But we are polluting the heavens and making blueprints for launching nuclear missiles from the sky. All because we live in fear. Can the Goddess tradition help us rediscover the beauty of the Living God? Can it persuade us to open our hearts? We have no alternative, it seems to me, than attempting to see if it can.

Inanna, Demeter, and Psyche

THE DARK HEART OF ANGER

The question that immediately poses itself to someone from the God-the-Father tradition reading the story of "Inanna's Descent"[1] is "Why is this Scripture?" Why was the story in which a hag-queen triumphs over a beautiful goddess included among the sacred writings of the Sumerians? There is a concession to the powers of darkness in this ancient myth that has no parallel in the God-the-Father tradition. And this is shocking. Here is the story. The goddess Inanna, mature and in full possession of her powers, resolves on a trip to the underworld. She adorns herself with jewels and instructs her servant Ninshubur to plead with the gods on her behalf should she not return. Encountering Neti, the gatekeeper to the underworld, she is asked the purpose of her visit. "I have come to witness the funeral rites [of] Guglananna, the husband of my older sister Ereshkigal,"[2] she replies. At this, Neti reports to Ereshkigal, who "slap[s] her thigh and bit[es] her lip"[3] and orders that Inanna be admitted to her realm after first being stripped. At each of the seven gates of the underworld, one of Inanna's adornments—including her crown and royal robe—is removed until finally, "naked and bowed low"[4] she enters the throne room of Ereshkigal. The judges of the underworld pronounce her guilty, while Ereshkigal gives her the evil eye. At a single blow from the hag-queen, Inanna is turned into a corpse and hung from a hook on the wall.

Meanwhile, Inanna's servant Ninshubur is making the rounds of the gods, asking for their help in rescuing his mistress. Only Enki, the god of the waters, the god of wisdom, is sympathetic. He fashions two creatures small enough to slip through the cracks of the underworld and gives them the food and water of life. He tells them that Ereshkigal lies naked and moaning—"with the cries of a woman about to give birth"[5]— and that they are to go and moan with her. In the underworld, they echo Ereshkigal's cries until she stops and offers them a gift. Requesting the corpse of Inanna, they sprinkle the food and water of life on it and Inanna arises. Immediately attempting to leave the underworld, Inanna is seized by the underworld judges. "No one ascends from the underworld unmarked,"[6] they declare and tell Inanna that if she wishes to return to the "Great Above," she must provide someone to take her place in the "Great Below." As Inanna ascends, demons cling to her. Accompanying her from place to place, they suggest first Ninshubur and then both of Inanna's sons as possible replacements for her in the underworld. In each case, she rejects their proposal. Finally, they find her consort Dumuzi who is sitting "on his magnificent throne"[7] by the big apple tree in Uruk. Inanna "fasten[s] on Dumuzi the eye of death . . . utter[s] against him the word of guilt" and cries, "Take him! Take Dumuzi away!"[8] The Sumerian text breaks off shortly after this.

To ask about the sacred character of the Inanna story is to ask about the value of anger. The triumph of Ereshkigal over Inanna signifies nothing so much as the ascendancy of rage in the personality. And we must be clear about where this rage comes from. We have already surmised that some altercation with Dumuzi seems to have provoked it, but the intensity suggests that it comes from the archaic layer of Inanna's psyche— where the age-old resentment of women towards men is stored.

Patriarchy had been in place for centuries when this story was written; imagine the resentment toward men and male gods that women must have been hoarding. The sacredness of anger, in this story, lies not in the anger itself, but in that it is *revealed*. A beautiful goddess identified with a hag-queen— isn't the story saying that Inanna and Ereshkigal are linked, that Ereshkigal is precisely the other side, the dark side of Inanna? Men would naturally relate to this revelation in terror: woman, the life-giver, could be cruel and their previous awe at her life-giving powers would have heightened their dread of her cruelty. But women would have perceived Inanna's anger differently. To feel one's anger is to feel oneself *completed* as a person. It is to know oneself as having an *archaic* layer, something deeper than what appears on the surface. Worse than being capable of cruelty is a woman identifying only with what she is on the surface.

Let us probe more deeply the source of Inanna's anger. We have said that it is the age-old resentment of women towards men. As such, it has to be due to women's powerlessness. A powerless person is angry not because she holds a subordinate role in society, for one's social role is not essential to what one is, but because she is treated by others as though she *were* defined by that role. There is an ontological injustice committed here. People in power have no right to treat others as though they existed for them. The powerless person senses that, but feels helpless to assert herself, to live *for herself*, without the affirmation of that self by another. Human beings "have the power," Beverly Harrison declares, "not only to create personal bonds between people but, more basically, to build up and deepen *personhood itself*."[9] When a woman rages against her powerlessness, she is asserting herself and she cherishes her rage for that reason. Ereshkigal's rage, however, is directed toward Inanna, which suggests that our initial tendency is to turn our anger *against* ourselves. Instead of being a cry of self-assertion, it is the hiss of self-hatred. This is because, until I am affirmed by another, I cannot affirm anything about myself, not even or especially not, my justified anger. Hence, I turn it against the object I have been taught, if only indirectly, to despise: myself. First of all, I hate myself for being powerless.

Inanna-Ereshkigal appears to be caught in a vicious circle. A victim of the injustice of not being recognized, she is angry, but because she is not recognized and thus lacks the ability to assert herself, she cannot find the proper focus for her anger and turns it on herself, reinforcing her sense of her own wretchedness. When you hate yourself, you want to destroy everything about yourself that is beautiful, that makes you attractive and desirable to others. You take a grim satisfaction in divesting yourself of all your adornments—the way Ereshkigal is gleeful in anticipating the stripping of Inanna. The pleasure seems to derive from the exercise of power the self-stripping amounts to, from its imitation of the powerful figures that have hurt you through abuse and neglect. The cost of this dark use of power, however, is enormous. Closing your heart against yourself cuts off the flow of what Simone Weil calls "vital energy"[10]—what we are calling the life-force—through your being so that your experience of life becomes flat. The feeling tone is absent from all your experiences and performing the activities necessary to sustain life begins to seem scarcely worth the effort. The pleasure of a perverse exercise of power gives way very quickly to despair. In the myth, the next time Ereshkigal appears, after casting the evil eye against Inanna and killing her, she is moaning in pain.

When active self-hatred gives way to despair, we can say that the circle of the self is broken, for despair is the inability to relate to oneself, as Kierkegaard says,[11] to close the circle of self-relation. (Self-hatred, we should note, however perverse, is a type of self-relation.) If self-relation, as a definite standpoint, provides perspective in one's life, the lack of it in despair would amount to the absence of perspective and the corresponding experience of disorientation, where all focus and direction to one's life are gone. To despair is to lose the future. The program of self-hatred is at least a program; to despair is to have no program. We can go so far as to say that a person in despair is on the verge of madness, if we understand madness as the takeover of the dark forces in the personality—symbolized in the myth by Ereshkigal's demons—made possible by the absence of self-relation. Self-relation normally holds the dark forces at bay; without it, one is susceptible to self-destructive urges and promptings. (I once knew a man who heard voices telling him that he was no good, that no one, not even God could love him. What I remember about this man is that it was impossible to have a coherent conversation with him. His thoughts seemed to come from all directions at once, for he had no defining center from which to look out upon the world.) Self-relation is a place. The pain of despair is being no place, displaced from one's center of control.

The least helpful advice you can give to a person in despair is to tell her to pull herself together. The lack of self-relation is such an energy drain that even self-hatred, which may have been habitual—is an effort. The wise person—and this is Ianna's grandfather Enki in the myth—knows to do the simpler thing of acknowledging, of recognizing the other's pain. Enki's little creatures merely echo Ereshkigal's cries as she lies naked and disheveled. Yet their sympathy brings her back to herself and immediately afterwards, Inanna revives. There is a miracle of healing portrayed here, something which may happen countless times without our noticing it, but which is a wondrous thing nonetheless. A person on the brink of madness, on the verge of losing her self-integrity, is brought back. It is so simple: Ereshkigal is able to relate to herself again because someone took the time to relate to her. For the time being, at least, the circle of herself is closed and her beautiful face reappears. We get the idea that Inanna's return is not something that Ereshkigal consciously wills. Rather, she instinctively responds to the sympathetic understanding of Enki's creatures. It appears that the desire to live or life-force is innate. Despair eclipses this desire. But if someone can come between us and ourselves—forge the missing link in the circle of our self-relation—the desire to live is released.

The release of one's desire to live—this is the first experience of heart's release that we encounter in the tradition of underworld journeys. Reflected upon, it would appear as a moment of grace, for as important as the will is, it is not effected by an act of will: the upsurge of desire comes from a deeper region than the will governs. Inanna, however, being unreflective, is not humbled by the experience of heart's release. Instead of marveling at her rescue, she returns to the land of the living with a vengeance. In tapping her desire to live, she knows she is drawing on a powerful energy source and she is determined to use that power to her own advantage. There was a moment on her journey when she could have returned as a different Inanna—not simply aware of the power of the desire to live in her but, out of gratitude, willing to exercise that power for others as well as herself. When the little creatures sympathized with her, she could have felt her equality with them, realizing that we are all connected through the same life-force. Instead she claims the power of life for herself. This is indicated by her protection of those closest to her— her servant and her sons—from the underworld demons and her focusing of her wrath on Dumuzi, her original antagonist. If Inanna would have returned from the underworld grateful, Dumuzi would have been spared. Feeling her connection with others extending to him would have diffused her anger. But Inanna is at the point of relishing her anger and letting it find what is for her its proper object.

We have come across something important in interpreting the Inanna story: the heart's release does not necessarily lead to generosity or largeness of heart. Rather, everything depends on how one relates to that experience. Like Inanna, we can simply claim the power that is released—whether that be the desire to live, sexual desire, or some other power—in which case, we simply become more powerful or we can let it awaken us to the mystery which is at the source of the powers. The second case leads to humility and a willingness to share the power that has been released in us with others. Instead of evoking awareness of what we might call "the holy mystery," Inanna's story simply portrays the numinosity of power. Why should we think that there *is* a source of the powers, a holy mystery from which they issue rather than a nothingness which would make them all random forces in the void? The answer is simply that to the attentive heart, the upsurge of life-giving power in one's being appears as gracious gift, not as randomness. Inanna's heart is not attentive, she is too intent on wielding power to reflect on its source. But isn't she like all of us in this? Don't we all desire to one day be powerful in relation to those who oppress us? The value of "Inanna's Descent" is that it reminds us of where we begin, on the spiritual journey—with a heart so enthralled by power that it is impervious to the grace of the heart's release.

Inanna's return, however vindictive, does represent a gain in terms of her self-possession. From self-hatred and despair, she has progressed to a sense of self-worth strong enough that she can confront Dumuzi for his abuse or neglect of her. It is self-respecting to vent our anger against someone who has done us harm. This is something that the God-the-Father tradition does not recognize sufficiently. If certain thinkers in that tradition affirm the notion of righteous anger, it is not a concept that has been communicated effectively to believers. Only God the Father has a right to be angry, according to popular thinking; his subjects must submit to whatever befalls them as proper acquiescence to His will. In attacking Dumuzi, Inanna is renouncing the stance of passivity in the face of wrong-doing that does violence to the one who is passive. Anger at injustice is heartfelt; anytime we suppress that anger, we drive a wedge between ourselves and our own hearts. Pretty soon, we are out of touch with what we really know and feel. Our thinking mimics what those in power think, rather than being an expression of genuine convictions. Expressing anger at Dumuzi is actually healing for Inanna in that it closes the gap between her and her heart. When she cries, "Take him, take Dumuzi away!" it is Ereshkigal's voice that we hear though it is Inanna who is speaking. This proves that Inanna is in touch with her heart—the dark heart of her anger—and that she is respecting herself and Dumuzi by expressing it.

What would it take for a powerless person to become compassionate? The Inanna story is not helpful on this point, for it leaves us with Inanna wielding her newfound power against her husband. The story is a caution to us against thinking that one can move from powerlessness to compassion without passing through anger. Anger inevitably chokes one's heart when one is powerless and the first step in becoming heart-free and capable of relating to others with an open heart is to express that anger. Anger expressed is at least a heartfelt communication. Trying to love someone—as the God-the-Father tradition too often would have us do—toward whom we harbor a deep resentment is an exercise in self-deception. Denying our resentment and "being nice" to the other only reinforces the split within ourselves that makes authentic action impossible. Yet expressing one's anger, however necessary, is hardly a desirable term for the underworld journey. The myth leaves us with the sense that Inanna wielding her power, while more fully herself, is ruthless. She is determined to go to any length to remain powerful and so she resists the vulnerability that allowed Dumuzi to hurt her. Inanna returned from the underworld is a woman who has hardened her heart. Is it possible to be both powerful and compassionate? Can we free ourselves of our anger without losing our self-respect? Centuries after "Inanna's Descent," another myth appeared which can help us answer these questions.

THE GENTLE HEART OF COMPASSION

With "Demeter and Persephone," we enter a different world than that of Inanna. Inanna's realm is that of instinct, of the desire to live as a kind of craving of the body, while

Demeter's is that of feeling. If the story were really about a mother and daughter, we would find, surely, maternal instinct at its center. But Persephone is not so much Demeter's daughter as her maidenhood. Indeed, the three goddesses in the myth—Persephone, Demeter, and Hecate—represent what the ancients took to be the three aspects of woman: maid, mother, and crone. At the end of the story, all the goddesses come together. The myth would seem to be about woman's wholeness: its lack in a woman's life when maiden and mother are split apart and its attainment when they are reunited. Wholeness has to do with how one feels about oneself; it implies a sense of peace rather than conflict—the feeling that opposing aspects of the self are complementary rather than at odds. Maid and mother are opposing figures in a woman's psyche. They correspond to the difference between being carefree and having a care. When Demeter is searching for Persephone, she is grieving the loss of her child-likeness: her spontaneity, her creativity, her playful abandon. The care she represents is heavy, exclusive of joy. But when Demeter and Persephone come back together, what is symbolized is a quality of care that is light-hearted, that is compatible with freedom of thought and emotion.

The story begins with Persephone playing in a sunlit meadow.[12] She has just reached down to smell the fragrance of a beautiful blossom when Hades, "with his immortal horses," bursts through the earth to seize her and take her back to the underworld. Frantic at hearing her daughter's cries, Demeter searches for her like a wild woman—stopping neither for food nor rest. At the end of nine days, the goddess Hecate comes to Demeter bearing a torch. She guides the mother to Helios, who tells Demeter to take heart, saying that it is Zeus who has arranged the marriage between her daughter and Hades. Darkening at this discovery, Demeter abandons the assembly of the gods on Mount Olympus and begins to roam among the "cities of men." Worn out with grief—her goddess nature completely eclipsed—she comes to the well at Eleusis, where she meets the king's daughters. They invite her to the palace, saying that their mother is seeking a nursemaid for her infant son. Demeter is a skilled nurse for the baby boy Demophoon, but at night, with the idea of making him immortal, she plunges him into the fire. Caught one night by the boy's mother, who screams at Demeter to stop, the goddess becomes enraged and reveals for the first time her divine nature. She orders the awestruck onlookers to build her a temple. When the goddess withdraws into her temple, the land suffers a blight. Over the whole earth, not a tree or plant bears fruit. Alarmed, Zeus send the gods to placate her and finally orders Persephone's release. When Demeter emerges from her temple, mother and daughter are reunited. Persephone tells her mother that she has eaten the seed of the pomegranate that Hades gave her which means, her mother says, that she will have to return to the underworld for a part of every year. Joined by Hecate, mother and daughter, rejoicing, take their places in the assembly of the gods.

Being carefree versus having a care. At no time do these two aspects of a woman come into conflict more violently than in a time of stress such as when she is contemplating a serious commitment: getting married, having a child, undertaking a major project. The conflict announces itself through the feeling of anxiety. There is the sense of a void at the center of yourself, as if something essential to the self were lacking. Every time you are alone, you are aware of the void and your anxiety can become excruciating. Meanwhile, what appears to consciousness, as if the void were a manufacturer of false selves—are two opposing figures: a child-woman and a dark woman. The child does everything she can to flee the void—swooning emotionally, conversing incessantly—both with others and in an ongoing interior monologue—eating or drinking or sleeping away the hours. In the myth Persephone's intoxication with the bloom of narcissus leads me to believe that she was equally willing to be intoxicated by Hades—that the violence on his part was met by abandonment on hers.

The dark woman, on the other hand, is a kind of menacing figure—Hecate, in the Demeter and Persephone story, she is Ereshkigal's descendant. Hecate was the goddess of the crossroads and this figure must be reckoned with at every crisis. She stands between a woman and the void, projecting fear and jealousy when shunned, becoming the purveyor of intuitive wisdom when befriended. Tension between Persephone (the child-woman) and Hecate (the dark woman) is not intrinsic; it appears when a woman faces the crisis of commitment.

The myth assumes that woman is mother, which is to say that having a care is what defines her. Having a care—opening the circle of yourself and letting it close around the man you love, the child you are carrying, or the work God wants you to carry out. This is what we mean by investing your self, making a real commitment. A woman is apt to do this unconsciously when she falls in love, conceives a child, or has laid on her heart some work to be accomplished. Her commitment becomes conscious precisely at the moment that it seems to cost the loss or death of the child-woman in her—her eager sexuality, her delicious abandonment to all things beautiful and sensual. A woman awakens from her sensual dreaminess only through a shock. "I thought you all glittering, with the noblest of carriage," Anna Livia Plurabelle says in James Joyce's *Finnegans Wake*, "you're only a bumpkin. I thought you the great in all things, in guilt and glory. You're but a puny."[13] For many women the realization that the man they love is different—is less—than what they had thought him to be can be extremely disillusioning. Their sense of self is deflated. Where once they were identified with a prince—which allowed their child-woman the most voluptuous fantasies—now they find themselves stuck with someone drearily ordinary. No wonder Demeter is frantic when she first becomes aware of the loss of Persephone. When the child-woman disappears from a woman's life, it seems that all loveliness is gone with her.

The disappearance of the child-woman forces a woman—perhaps for the first time—to take the dark woman, the crone, for an ally. Before this, she may have been unable to sit still and reflect. The child-woman can sit still, but she loses herself in daydreams, never bringing her thoughts to bear on her actual situation. Awareness of the void propels her outside of herself. Befriending the dark woman means waiting at the spot—the spot where one actually stands—for knowledge of what to do next. What we are looking for is a glimmer of meaning to chart our way through disillusionment. If one refused to befriend the crone at this juncture, she could take over the personality in a negative way, like Inanna become Ereshkigal. But if one waits—and waiting is hard for it means waiting in the dark, the antithesis of the sunlit meadow the child loved—meaning can be discerned. When Hecate comes to Demeter bearing a torch, what is symbolized is the intuitive sense that there *is* a meaning to her daughter's sudden disappearance. When Demeter and Hecate find out from Helios that Zeus had arranged the abduction, meaning is confirmed. Yet Demeter is not ready to find out *what* meaning there is in the loss of her daughter. Her pain has created a resentment of Zeus that blocks the attainment of insight. Instead, she strikes out in a new direction—determining to forge her own meaning for her life.

Forging a meaning versus waiting for meaning to reveal itself. When we have suffered a loss, it can be very difficult to wait in the pain of loss for the discovery of meaning. Instead, action—any action that removes the focus from the pain— seems preferable. Leaping into a new sphere of action—like Demeter abandoning Mount Olympus for the "cities of men"— seems most desirable. The appeal of action is that it gives us the sense of being in control of our lives despite the calamity that has come to pass. Disillusionment, pain, loss are signs of the lack of control we have over our lives. As such, they throw us into a panic until some order, some control has been restored. But when Demeter imposes a new order *of her own making*, she is guilty, like Inanna, of missing an occasion of grace. It is one thing for a woman to befriend the dark woman in herself, to rely on that intuitive sense that can come to our aid in times of crisis. It is another to wait for a revelation from the void. We have said that the dark woman stands between a woman and the void. Our intuitive sense is not our deepest source of knowledge. The void is deeper. Anyone who has even glimpsed it knows that however dreadful it appears, it is also pregnant with possibility. Yet who can summon the courage to befriend the void? Like Demeter, we can be certain that there *is* meaning to be discerned in a loss we are suffering, but lack the receptivity of heart, the willingness to go deep into ourselves to find out what it is.

The sterility of forging a way of one's own choosing as opposed to following a way that is revealed is what is symbolized, it seems, by Demeter's misadventures with Demophoon. He is a substitute for her missing child. As we all do with the way we have substituted for the true way we could have discovered, Demeter tries to force Demophoon to be more than he is. To admit that the way we have chosen fails to engage our heart is too painful. It raises again the specter of the void and of one's life being out of control. So it is natural to attempt to shape a meaningful life through sheer effort of will. "Perhaps you cannot imagine what it means to see your whole life ahead of you and to form a firm and constant resolution to make something of it, to steer it from beginning to end by your will and effort in a special direction."[14] Simone Weil, the French philosopher/ mystic, wrote this in a letter to a friend when she was contemplating a move from teaching to work in a factory, a change that she was sure would further strengthen her will. In Simone Weil's obsession with testing herself, constantly seeking out ordeals to endure, obstacles to overcome, we can see that the exercise of one's will can become a fanatical preoccupation. From being carefree, a person can make the transition to caring with a vengeance—exerting control over her life as if an unseen enemy were threatening to subvert it.

What the myth brings out is that the unseen enemy for every woman who has awakened from her sensual dreaminess is death. It is death that fills us with dread, that makes us aware of the void at the center of ourselves. A woman who is denying death can still have dreams about it. I remember a dream in which I was a child playing in a sunlit meadow—just like Persephone. I reached down to pick a beautiful flower and when I lifted it to my face found that its underside was covered with maggots. I have also dreamed of death as a huge black dog that was trying to break through a door I was holding shut. Awareness of death—conscious or subconscious—and the crisis of commitment seem to go together. It is precisely the awareness of death, awareness of the void that makes us want to commit ourselves to someone or something. Death makes me realize that what I do with my life *matters*—that to live without direction or purpose is unworthy. Yet the myth indicates that to force a commitment, to seize on the first path that presents itself instead of waiting for my true path to emerge, is a mistake. Zeus had plans for Demeter, but in choosing to ignore them, she gets into trouble. The next step, if Demeter wants to go forward in her life, can only be a confrontation with Zeus.

The question arises, if the way Demeter should follow has been foreordained by Zeus, how can we identify it as her true path, i.e., the way she can follow in freedom of mind and heart? To follow a way ordained by Zeus, as opposed to a way of her own choosing, would seem to be an act of self-coercion, the willful submission of herself to an alien will. In the rage that erupts when Demeter is prevented from putting the infant Demophoon into the fire, we are reminded of Inanna's attack on Dumuzi, which concludes the story of her descent. Yet Demeter's story does not end, as Inanna's does, with an expression of anger. Instead, and this is the beginning of the answer to our question, she withdraws into herself—this is what is symbolized by Demeter withdrawing into the temple—to a point that is deeper than the blade of her anger. Demeter's anger flares up again, after her time in the temple (when she finds that Persephone has eaten the seed of the pomegranate) but from then on, it no longer determines her. Demeter emerged from her temple is a woman who has transcended her anger: without denying it, she is able to live and act from a deeper level than that carved out by anger. What this means is that she can be reconciled with Zeus—for the story ends with her return to Mt. Olympus—and that a willing rather than a willful submission to his will is possible.

Our question becomes, what transpires when Demeter is in the temple? It is a confrontation with Zeus as well as a withdrawal into herself, for Zeus is alarmed by her sudden withdrawal. To withdraw to a place deeper than the anger in yourself is to admit, to full consciousness, the void; it is to come face to face with death. At that moment, we realize that death is the god we really worship, the power that holds us in thrall, for it is impossible to face death without cringing. Facing death is also facing God because death is God's destroying arm. The author of life must also, inevitably, be in control of death. To face death is to discover what is signified in the myth by Hades—God's dark side. In the first instance, this is a purifying discovery. It removes every trace of our efforts to image God in terms of our standards of goodness. Death and the good, to our ordinary ways of thinking, are incompatible. There is a second moment in our encounter with the void, but Demeter doesn't wait for it. Instead, the awesomeness of her discovery—of the power of death and the reality of God's dark side—elicit an about-face from her. What happens in the temple is that Demeter relents, like Job before the majesty of the Living God. She forswears her anger because she sees that death is unavoidable; the destroying arm of God *is*. The myth portrays, of course, only the relenting of Zeus—in his dispatching of a messenger to the nether world to order the release of Persephone. But we know that in the darkness of her temple, it is Demeter who first relents, because in real life, it is only our relenting that brings about the relenting of God. That is a strange phrase—the relenting of God—and yet it is true to experience. When you are up against death, your heart paralyzed with fear, if you can get it to open as much as a crack (and this is what we mean by relenting—opening your heart), the God of life and death seems to change. The heart glows as it opens and for a moment, I seem to perceive the mystery of God from within. In that moment, I know that God's face might be dreadful, but His nature is all compassion. In that meeting, I discover the well of compassion in me. It springs from God's compassion and reveals that at the very center of myself, God and I are joined. When a woman makes this discovery, she forgives God for everything—like Job, we can imagine, coming to forgive God for his open sores and the loss of his children and all his earthly possessions. To forgive God is to be able to make a new beginning in one's life—to be able to accept what is given without hankering for another way, the perfect way. When you draw on your well of compassion, every encounter is a heartfelt encounter; the ordinary events of your life are resonant. The secret of wholeness, it seems, is to be in touch with the center of yourself, to have access to the well of compassion that lies at the center and to draw on it. At the center, the split between the child-woman and the mother is healed. Being carefree and having a care no longer conflict in the personality, but are complementary. The whole woman, through the power of compassion, claims both the child and the mother as aspects of herself. And so I discover that neither the child, nor the mother, nor the old wise woman—the crone—essentially defines me, for at the center, I am infinite. My power to relate to the things of my life, to the different aspects of myself, is unconditioned. The unconditioned, in me, is spirit and from the center, I can see that the conflict I experienced was due to a trammeling of my spirit, an attempt to limit myself to this or that when, on account of spirit, I am unlimited—not this and not that. The freedom experienced at this standpoint is what makes it possible to accept the way that is given, in one's life, the way on which one finds oneself—and to accept it gratefully. In the freedom of spirit, we are grateful to be and one's

physical ailments, one's oppressive situation, one's heart-aches
limit but do not negate one's freedom. "Pain is the color of
certain events," Simone Weil says.[15] She seems to mean that
the freedom of spirit allows us to be aware of pain, to experience pain, but to live from a place beyond it.

The whole woman who has emerged in my interpretation of the Demeter-Persephone story is a far cry from
the angry woman who finds her voice at the conclusion of
"Inanna's Descent." Demeter is at peace with her life as she
rejoins the gods and goddesses on Mount Olympus, whereas
Inanna is still raging against it. From the standpoint of wholeness, we can see that times of darkness and confusion recur
in a life—in the imagery of the myth, Persephone again and
again departs to the underworld. But we can anticipate these
times without anxiety, for we have discovered the "still point"
in ourselves where we can be at peace, whatever our life situation. By drawing on the well of compassion, it is possible to
remain open to others, during dark times and to exult, from
one's inmost self, over beauty. The woman who never lets go
of her anger and does not find the well of compassion never
recovers the child in herself. Her creativity, her spontaneity,
her instinctual appetites are all blocked. But when the mother's
burden of care becomes the power of compassion, the different aspects of a woman alternate—as the situation demands—
in a kind of dance. Darkness calls forth the old wise woman—
the power of intuition—just as sunlit meadows evoke one's
child. The whole woman in us knows, like the author of
Ecclesiastes, the seasons of a life and she can respond to each
in its turn without losing herself.

The emergence of the whole woman brings us to a new
understanding of the meaning of commitment. When it is
the weightiness of care that defines me, commitment means
to be identified with the person or thing to which I have
opened the circle of myself and made part of my self-relation.
In this case, a woman's connection to the other determines
her state of mind. In a marriage, for example, a woman may

be so identified with her partner that she instinctively re-joices when he rejoices—whatever the cause of his rejoicing—and grows heavy-hearted when he is depressed. The line be-tween self and other blurs. While many people seem to be seeking just this kind of fusion with another self, the truth is that the nature of this relationship precludes compassion. Compassion for the other requires that, first of all, she recog-nize him as other and not as an extension of herself. As other, the person exists for himself, with his own life and his own point of view, before he exists for her. In identifying with him, she denies the inviolability of his unique stand-point. When she has found her center and can identify, not with another and with her care for him or her, but with her-self and spirit in herself, in compassion, she can release the other to live for himself. She is able to relate to the other not out of need—the need to be shielded from the void, perhaps—but freely.

Authentic commitment must have its basis in freedom. What is the focus for my life when I am no longer determined by care? In my relationships with another, my new focus is the whole person in him—as realized or as trying to emerge. I lis-ten for the voice of the whole person in what he says and watch for signs of the whole person in what he does. When the whole person has not emerged or is eclipsed in him, I wait. What devotion could be more worthy than this? In encoun-tering the whole person in my partner, I am brought back to my own center and to the freedom of that standpoint. I can feel my needs—and feel them intensely, at times—but they do not intrude on the circle of our relating. Can a relationship—an intimate relationship like that of husband and wife—really be this pure? The Demeter-Persephone myth warns us—through the symbolism of Persephone's annual return to the underworld—against assuming that the discovery of whole-ness is once-and-for-all. Instead, we seem to have glimpses of wholeness—moments of real mutuality—as we struggle to break our restrictive patterns of relating to each other. A need to identify with another person, preferably someone perceived as greater or more powerful, can be so ingrained as to be instinctive. The thrall of the instincts is not undone by the simple discovery of wholeness. The Demeter-Persephone myth leaves us with the question, but does not itself reveal how wholeness might become instinctive.

THE PASSIONATE HEART OF LOVING

From falling in love—and living in a sensual paradise—to entering the spiritual paradise of loving—that is the story of Eros and Psyche.[16] The difference between falling in love and loving is portrayed in the myth by the contrast between an enchanted castle, where Eros visits Psyche only at night, and the heaven to which she is borne by her lover in the light of day, where she herself becomes immortal. Between these two moments of the myth is an account of sheer travail. Psyche suffers despair and contemplates suicide; she is set to impossible tasks and endures the ordeal of a journey through the underworld. The myth invites us to reflect, then, on the connection between love and suffering. While falling in love seems to be something that "just happens" to us, loving, according to the myth, is the fruit of suffering willingly undergone. More than any art or skill, loving involves a radical openness of the self; it requires the painful transformation of one's subconscious mind. As her name indicates, Psyche represents the soul, which is first of all dark, because unknown to our conscious minds. Her journey represents the integration of soul—its emergence as a real power in our lives.

Psyche is the most beautiful woman in the world, we are told, so beautiful that people were starting to worship her and neglecting Aphrodite. The goddess, of course, is angry at this and instructs her son Eros to inflame Psyche with a passion for the "vilest of men."[17] Meanwhile, for all her beauty, Psyche lacks suitors. Men are so in awe of her that they treat her "like a statue"[18] rather than a flesh and blood woman. Her father appeals to Apollo for insight into his daughter's fate and learns that she must be taken to a mountain top and left there to be ravished by a beast. The beast, however, turns out to be Eros whose love for Psyche prevents him from carrying out his mother's bidding. He visits the girl by night in a magnificent palace to which she has been carried by the west wind. Psyche's bliss with Eros is soon disturbed by the news that her sisters are mourning her death. She pleads with Eros for a chance to visit them and he relents, enjoining her strictly not to reveal his identity. "For soon we shall have issue," he says, "and even now your womb, a child's as yet, bears a child like to you. If you keep my secret in silence, he shall be a god; if you divulge it, a mortal."[19] Her sisters' grief turns to envy when Psyche appears to them. They tell her that her husband is really a loathsome serpent and urge her to take lantern and knife and kill him in his sleep. When the lantern shines on Eros, Psyche is overcome by a new ecstasy of love and covers the god with kisses. Eros awakes and flies off, leaving Psyche to wander aimlessly, throwing herself into a river, at one point, in her despair.

Counseled by the god Pan to cease despairing and search for Eros, Psyche begins a long journey. She visits the homes of her sisters and through trickery, takes revenge on them. Next, she seeks refuge, first, in the temple of Demeter and then in Hera's temple. Both goddesses send her on her way, claiming loyalty to their sister Aphrodite. Finally, Psyche decides to submit to the great goddess who is ransacking heaven and earth to find Psyche and punish her. In Aphrodite's house, Psyche is greeted by a "wild laugh"[20] and a beating from the goddess. Then she is put through a series of trials. Ordered to sort a heap of seeds by nightfall, Psyche is first overwhelmed by the task, then watches gratefully as an army of ants does the work for her. Her next challenge is to collect the golden fleece from some wild rams. Once again, Psyche contemplates suicide, but this time, a green reed comes to her rescue. She follows the reed's advice to hide from the rams until afternoon, when they are sleeping and she can gather strands of wool from trees in the grove where they pasture. Aphrodite's next test is to determine whether Psyche has "a stout heart and prudence beyond the prudence of women."[21] She is to fill a crystal urn with the water of death that flows from a mountain peak. Providence intervenes once more and an eagle carries out the task for her.

The story reaches its climax in Psyche's trip through the underworld. Ordered by Aphrodite to go to Persephone's realm and bring back some of the goddess's beauty, Psyche marches instead to a high tower, thinking to leap to her death. The tower warns her that by entering the underworld this way, she will not return and instructs her in the rules for a safe passage through the land of the dead. Psyche takes heart and obeys the rules—ignoring the entreaties of a lame man, a dead man, and some old weaving women, paying Charon his ferryman's toll, throwing a cake of barley to the three-headed hound at Persephone's threshold, and refusing to eat the rich foods the goddess sets out for her. The tower's last warning was against opening the casket containing Persephone's treasure. On regaining "the shining daylight,"[22] Psyche succumbs to this last temptation. Desirous of making herself more beautiful for Eros, she opens the casket. Instead of beauty, out flows a Stygian sleep which makes the girl unconscious. But Eros, recovered from his wound from the oil in Psyche's lamp, wipes away the sleep and bears his beloved off to heaven. There, with Zeus's approval, the two are joined in marriage. Psyche is offered a goblet of ambrosia as Zeus proclaims, "Psyche, drink of this and be immortal. Then Eros shall never leave your arms, but your marriage shall endure forever."[23] Shortly after the wedding, the story concludes, Psyche gives birth to a baby girl whose name, "in the language of mortals,"[24] is Pleasure.

The sensual paradise of Psyche's enchanted castle seems a world away from the heaven she enters with Eros, yet we misunderstand the experience of falling in love if we fail to see in the former an intimation of the latter. What distinguishes falling in love from mere attraction is the element of transcendence: to fall in love is to encounter the other as mysterious, as holding the key to what Proust calls, "the mysterious life."[25] However dazzling the beauty of the other, however familiar his or her face becomes, in real love there is this kernel of darkness, of the unknown. About the experience of soulful love, D. H. Lawrence writes,

> Rare women wait for the re-born man. For the lotus, as you know, will not answer to all the bright heat of the sun. But she curves her dark, hidden head in the depths, and stirs not. Till, in the night, one of these rare, invisible suns that have been killed and shine no more, rises among the stars in unseen purple, and like the violet, sends its rare, purple rays out into the night. To these the lotus stirs as to a caress, and rises upward through the flood, and lifts up her bent head, and opens with an expansion such as no other flower knows, and spreads her sharp rays of bliss, and offers her soft, gold depths such as no other flower possesses, to the penetration of the flooding, violet-dark sun that has died and risen and makes no show. But for the golden brief day-suns of show such as Anthony, and for the hard winter suns of power, such as Caesar, the lotus stirs not, nor will ever stir. Those will only tear open the bud. Ah, I tell you, wait for the reborn and wait for the bud to stir.[26]

Before your soul is stirred, you lead a statue-like existence (like Psyche before her marriage to Eros). You may touch and be touched, but there is no quickening of that mysterious life that is your destiny.

Psyche's enchanted castle is a prison, of course. Her love of Eros enslaves her in that it causes her to live passively— awaiting the embrace of Eros and then receiving his embrace, in a perfectly predictable alternation. When a woman loves someone and is not rooted in herself, enchantment is inevitable. What sense of self she has she negates in order to be attuned to the other. She feels like a vessel that exists only to be filled by him or like an instrument that sings only to his touch. To a person with a developed sense of self, the abandonment of such an existence is horrifying, but to a Psyche—at least for awhile—it is a dream fulfilled. What determines the length of the stay in the enchanted castle is precisely the degree of self-awareness. If a woman is, however subconsciously, fleeing herself through abandonment to desire, her stay will be brief, interrupted almost immediately by the pangs of a destiny about to be missed. Psyche is sufficiently lacking in self-awareness that it takes the intervention of her sisters—those bitter embodiments of disillusionment in loving—to break free of her enchantment. As Erich Neumann in his extended commentary on the myth points out, the sisters, for all their ugliness, are essential to Psyche's development.[27] If the seeds of doubt in her lover's perfection are not planted in such a woman's mind, she may be doomed to the life of a devotee, never awakening to her own, intrinsic fire. The difference between tending someone else's fire and tending our own is striking. When a woman is a devotee, all her actions are for the purpose of tending her lover's fire—meeting his needs, reflecting his ideas back to him, thrilling at his expressions of desire. Her reward is a phosphorescent effect in her own life: some of his reflected energy glows in her. Apart from her lover, she grows listless and dull and so she perceives her need for him as vital; he makes her feel alive. As long as a woman is riveted by someone else's fire, she cannot begin to discover her own. Disillusionment with her lover and the dead space it creates are actually boons, for they can prompt her to look to herself. We have to think of Psyche's lamp and knife as symbolizing one of those moments of lucidity when a devotee recognizes her enslavement and lashes out against her lover. "What am I doing with my life?" she wails. The upsurge in Psyche of a greater passion for Eros at this point depicts the reversal that inevitably follows such truth-telling. When a woman is honest with her lover, as opposed to being nice or sweet or coy or seductive at the expense of honesty, the fire in herself blazes up. The incredible release this represents can express itself in wild love-making. The devotee, for once, is reveling in her own power, her own energy instead of that of her lover. But just as inevitably, the myth indicates, a man unaccustomed to truth-telling from a woman will take off. When a woman's own fire blazes up, such men tend to leave her alone.

Psyche's attempted suicide after Eros leaves her is typical of many women whose discovery of their own power scares off their lovers. A woman should revel and continue to revel in the fire of inspiration that she discovers in herself. She should value her clear-eyed vision of her devotion to her lover as enslavement. But she doesn't. The price of the spiritual breakthrough that this represents is the deep loneliness you feel when a myth you have lived by shatters. All a Psyche ever wants or thinks she wants is a life of devotion to a superior being. This is the myth inculcated in her by a society that worships power. In the shadow of such a being, she feels not eclipsed but secure—like a child who sleeps peacefully, trusting that her parents will protect her from any harm. The deep loneliness is not foreign to childhood, but it can be banished by a mother's embrace or a father's gently stroking hand. A patriarchal society allows women, indeed, encourages women to live by the myth its children live by—that all is well as long as you are in right relation, the relation of submission, to a father-figure. When she begins to doubt her lover's perfection and he flies off, Psyche cannot help but feel that all is not well, that she is exposed to danger from every side. In the loneliness—and anxiety—of this new standpoint, it is natural for a woman to sabotage her every move toward freedom.

There are two things that sustain Psyche in her first, halting steps away from the security of her idyll with Eros. The primary thing is her sense of destiny. The myth recounts that Psyche was emboldened to take lamp and knife against her lover "though flesh and spirit were weak and trembled," because "the fierce will of destiny gave her force."[28] There are times when we know that we must act, that we must take sword in hand and do the deed, come what may. Action severs us from what has gone before and gives us a new vantage point on the future. Sunk in her idyll, Psyche could only envision the future as more of the same. But once she acted or contemplated acting, it became fraught with possibility. The sense of destiny—that the action we are taking is meant—can nerve us to face possibility. A woman raised in a patriarchal society is likely to conceive of destiny, first of all, as the will of a cosmic father-figure for her life. Though this conception can bolster her ego, it precludes the possibility of real action, for it amounts to a continuation of her stance of submission and makes the future appear, not as possibility, but as a "deadly clear path"[29] to which she must simply conform. Psyche, interestingly (and unlike Demeter), gives no sign that she thinks of destiny as the inexorable will of Zeus for her life. Instead, it seems to be, for her, as even someone crippled by patriarchy can come to realize, the call—the demand—from the buried part of herself to be heard.

The second thing that keeps Psyche steadfast is the counsel of Pan. It is he who tells her, when she is trying to kill herself, to "cease from [her] grief and lay aside her sorrow and . . . address Eros, the mightiest of gods, with fervent prayer" so as to "win him by tender submission."[30] It is this advice which finally brings Psyche to Aphrodite's house and the showdown with the great goddess which results in her being reunited with Eros. The Pan-figure is someone particularly suited for mentoring women because his link to nature and the subterranean power of intuition gives him access to the feminine soul. A woman feels understood by such a person even before she begins to speak. When a woman's soul is buried, a Pan-figure can convey its wisdom to her, in effect, telling her what she knows but doesn't know that she knows. The fascination of a Pan-figure for a woman is the allure of her own soul conveyed by his speech. Her soul's beauty is so compelling that if she succumbs to his fascination, the spell can only be broken by extraordinary means. Psyche, of course, clings to Pan's words and not to him. Since she sends her sisters to their deaths in the next scene, we can see that his words overrule her inclination to disillusionment with Eros that the sisters embody. This is because they give voice to what Psyche, in her soul, has never doubted—that her love for Eros is not in vain, that if she persists in loving, through all hardships, there will come a time when it will flower.

Besides the fascination of a Pan-figure, there is another temptation to which a woman can succumb which will arrest her progress toward the reunion with her beloved that her soul seeks. This is the security provided by identification with one of the traditional roles for women, specifically, being a mother or being a wife. When Psyche seeks refuge, first in Demeter's and then in Hera's temple, what is being portrayed is the power of tradition to sidetrack a woman from her original desire. There is no harm—far from it—in a woman becoming a mother or becoming a wife. What is harmful is allowing the pleasures and duties of these roles to eclipse the soul's desire for freedom in loving. Without realizing it, a woman can allow the instincts to nurture and to mate to define her so that her freedom as a person is suppressed. Soul is personal; the instincts are impersonal. The woman who has integrated soul and the power of personhood that goes with it can relate freely to her roles as wife and mother. And the personal act of relating redeems the power of the instincts. When soul is unintegrated, instinctual desire seems to conflict with pure love. When soul is integrated, instinctual desire is love's expression.

We are beginning to see that Psyche's quest to be reunited with Eros is really a journey of self-liberation. A woman's instincts, reinforced by tradition, can be an irresistible force in her life. When she feels the loneliness of love's absence, the chill breeze that blows her way from the power of death newly exposed, it is hard, no, impossible, to refuse the security of an offer of marriage and the promise of children to fill her life. For a long time, it can seem that she is fulfilled by marriage and family, except for the disturbing sense she has that her voice, her true voice, has been muted. Perhaps in the night, her true voice cries out in her dreams, wailing for the love she has lost, for that intimation of transcendence that awakened her to a greater life. The life she is living, in conformity to the roles of wife and mother, seems so reduced, by comparison. She loves her husband, she loves her children, that is, she cares deeply for them, but she always remembers that other love, when her body flew in her lover's arms and she seemed to enter another world. The value of distance, on a lost love, is that the transcendent element crystallizes into an image that can inspire a personal quest. A woman may think: "However mired I am in my obligations as wife and mother, if I carry in my heart the image of a perfect love, my soul is not lost. By clinging to it, I remember that I am more than my roles, that I have a personal destiny." The memory of Eros that stirs Psyche to action we must understand as an image of pure transcendence, and therefore, an image of God.

When the image of a human lover is distilled into an image of God, he ceases to be a god in your life and becomes, instead, a mediating figure. We submit to a god, that is, we conform automatically to such a person's needs and expectations, but we strive to imitate one who mediates transcendence, who reveals to us the Living God. Whose heart does not respond to the beauty of a mediating figure? Who can refuse the quest his image inspires? In relation to such a person, we cannot doubt that our destiny is to become as beautiful as he is, that the power of personhood latent in us is to be realized. The beauty of a mediating figure is precisely the light of his undimmed personhood. Remembering a moment at a busy intersection in downtown Louisville when he was seized by an impulse of love for all the people milling around him, Thomas Merton writes, "There is no way of telling people that they are all walking around shining like the sun."[31] He goes on, "At the center of our being is a point of nothingness which is untouched by sin and by illusion, a point of pure truth, a point or spark which belongs entirely to God. . . . This little point of nothingness and of absolute poverty is the pure glory of God in us."[32] The concept of person is a mysterious concept. That is because the light or "spark" of which Merton speaks must be seen with the eyes of the soul to be known; it cannot be deduced. When we cherish the image of a mediating figure, our souls are learning to see.

The point of all Psyche's trials is that she learn to see in that region of darkness which the mind, on its own, cannot penetrate. What is more relevant to Psyche's quest, however, is that the region she explores is dreadful to the instincts. A Psyche, in the first place, lives by her instincts and not her mind. What she must overcome is not the mind's confusion when confronting the unknown, but the instincts' sheer terror. When Aphrodite beats Psyche—when the girl appears at her house before undertaking the tasks Aphrodite sets her— what is symbolized is the instincts' rebellion at the kind of journey Psyche is making. Aphrodite, the goddess of sexuality, represents the kind of love, if we can call it that, which relates to the unknown—the mystery of the other person— unknowingly. The blindness of instinctual love is indicated by its wanting to possess the other when the divine spark, which is love's true object, eludes possession. In her conflict with Aphrodite, Psyche symbolizes the person who is beginning to relate to the unknown knowingly, who is willing to forego possession of her lover in order to realize what she sees realized in him. From having to being—from having her lover to being like him—that is the transition Psyche's struggle with Aphrodite at this juncture represents. Instead of obeying the instincts' dread, which counsels retreat from the darkness they perceive, Psyche dares to trust that the light she associates with her lover's image will guide her through the darkness.

The significance of the tasks which Aphrodite assigns Psyche is that they are all impossible, that is, they can't be accomplished by Psyche's "own will and effort," as Simone Weil would put it. But this is precisely their value for her. When faced with an impossible task—like sorting a mountain of seeds, collecting the fleece from dangerous rams, bringing back an urn of water from the river of the dead—we are forced to rely on a power in ourselves that is other than that of will. This is the power which Simone Weil calls "attention," an attitude of receptivity to grace or inspiration to solve a particular problem.[33] While the power of willingness, prominently featured in the Demeter story, is unfocused, being the basic orientation of mind and heart that releases the flow of compassion, the power of attention, which presupposes willingness, is highly focused: its object is always the obstacle in the path, the problem that must be solved at this very moment. In being attentive, I am waiting for the flash of light that will illumine a patch of the unknown. Let us say that my impossible task is writing. Left to my "own will and effort," I produce nothing but wooden phrases out of the chaos of my thoughts. But when I give my attention to the subject to be articulated, that is, when I "suspend . . . [my] thought, leaving it detached, empty and ready to be penetrated by the object,"[34] as Simone Weil describes the process of attention, I find that my snarl of ideas takes a definite form. The power of attention seems to enkindle the divine spark in me which makes possible what was impossible to my "own will and effort."

The enkindling of the divine spark! What this way of describing the fruits of the practice of attention suggests is that the divine spark is, first of all, a glowing coal or ember that must be fanned before it bursts into flame. The element of transcendence is in all of us, but it shines forth only in those who consent to its emergence. The essence of attention is consent to being on fire. But we must be careful to distinguish a way of being from the flights of passion which attend falling in love. The connection between the two is clearly the divine spark, the element of transcendence which we first perceive in the other and only later—much later—begin to perceive in ourselves. The difference is the contrast between unknowing and knowing love which we have already seen. In a "flight of passion," my heart leaps in response to the other, but I don't know why. I am mystified by his effect on me. When I am engaged in a passionate existence, however, there is recognition. My heart still soars at the sight of my beloved, but now I recognize in him the same fire that burns in my own heart and I am in wonderment at the fire, not at him. A passionate existence—living by the fire in one's own heart— allows me to love the other intensely without making demands on him. "The great trouble of human life," Simone Weil says, "is that looking and eating are two different operations."[35] She seems to mean that when I first fall in love, I cannot look at the other without wanting to possess him and that my possessiveness degrades my love for him. But there comes a time, it seems, when looking and eating are not separate, when I see my beloved with the eyes of my soul and let my own fire be fed by my recognition of his.

But we are getting ahead of ourselves. Before Psyche's reunion with Eros, the greatest trial of all—a journey through the underworld—is required of her. The significance of Psyche's underworld journey—as distinguished from those portrayed in the Inanna and Demeter stories—is that Psyche remains herself through the experience: she does not metamorphose into a raging hag-queen, like Inanna, nor does she lose her childlike loveliness, which happens to Demeter. To remain ourself, in the face of the power of death, that is, to remain open to life instead of closing off and shutting down in anger and despair, requires letting go of all that death can take from us. Actually, the power of death strips us of everything we think we own; its darkness even eclipses the light of a mediating figure. So the choice we have is between relating to this operation willingly or unwillingly. At the prospect of an underworld journey, Psyche's first response is to despair, which is indicated by her intention of throwing herself from a high tower. Her particular anguish is that she must travel the underworld unsustained by the image of Eros, the image that had inspired her through all her previous trials. In his book, *The Lion, the Witch, and the Wardrobe*, C. S. Lewis refers to a "deep magic from the dawn of time" to which Aslan, the lion-king of Narnia, submits when he is put to death by the White Witch, Narnia's false queen.[36] The magic of death is powerful enough, apparently, to overshadow the good—in Psyche's case, to render ineffectual the power of her saving image.

In the absence of her lover's image, Psyche has only the tower's directions to guide her through the underworld. These are the standard precautions associated with underworld journeys, Erich Neumann tells us,[37] and they seem to serve the purpose of keeping Psyche from making contact with the spirits of the dead. Unclean spirits attach themselves readily to unsuspecting souls, that is, they prey on our fear and despair, whispering counsels of annihilation and self-annihilation until we seem to be doomed. But if we give them no purchase—"no sidelong glance, no furtive look, no encouragement of a dazzled fascination"[38] as I once wrote when I realized that my own love affair with death had run its course—then they have no power over us. The degree of one's susceptibility to the fascination of death and the spirits of the dead seems to be in reverse proportion to the degree to which one has integrated soul— the mysterious life glowing within oneself. Like any power, death is irresistibly fascinating until knowledge of our own power robs it of its coercive influence over us. Psyche is free relative to death and the spirits of the dead because she knows, after all her previous trials, that the same light that first blinded her in Eros exists in her. It will take the presence of her beloved for her to perceive that light in herself, but by its fruits, she is already assured that it is there.

The fruits of the integration of soul are simply knowing and loving—knowing or being able to recognize the divine spark in oneself and in others and loving with the flame of the divine spark. Knowing and loving can persist even when there has been an eclipse of the good in one's life—when we have no perception of the glory of God, as Thomas Merton calls it, either within ourselves or in others. At such times, that our arms still embrace the other willingly, that our hands reach out, unbidden, in a gesture of tenderness, is a sign that we have learned to see the soul of the other even in darkness, that its eclipse is no barrier to our love. What kind of miracle is this—that a soul enshrouded in darkness should still elicit my love? It is the miracle by which Psyche continues to love Eros, even though his power as a mediating figure for her is eclipsed. Think of it—an Eros who no longer serves as a mediating figure for Psyche is simply a man who has abandoned her. Yet unlike Inanna, who flies into a rage over Dumuzi's indifference and unlike Demeter, who closes her heart when the bloom of first love fades, Psyche remains open-hearted and it is this ability of hers which produces the miracle. A heart that is open, even in the dark, can see in the dark and what Psyche sees is a beautiful soul whose light is eclipsed. As she thinks of Eros, her love for him becomes like a wound, for it is painful to love a soul that is without light.

How do we distinguish Psyche's painful love of Eros from a self-destructive attachment to him? The myth is helpful on this point for in its portrayal of Psyche's rejection of the rich food of Persephone, it suggests precisely the kind of attachment that Psyche's love for Eros is not. To eat another's food is to have a kind of intercourse with that person, so to eat the food of Persephone, queen of the underworld, would be to have a kind of intercourse with death. The power of death, we have seen, is a very dangerous power in that it stirs up the forces of destruction in us. To have intercourse with death would be to abandon oneself to those forces, to revel in an orgy of annihilation and self-annihilation. Simone Weil speaks of an "infernal joy."[39] To the soul who feels abandoned to the powers of darkness, the power of death, that is, who cannot face death with the knowledge of her own beauty and power, there is a thrill in abandoning oneself to the power of death simply because—in contrast to one's ordinary sense of powerlessness—it gives one a sense of power. Psyche's attachment to Eros would be degrading if it represented an abandonment to the feelings of self-doubt and self-loathing that are always stirred up by another's rejection, as if remaining identified with Eros were the only way that she could feel worthwhile. But Psyche's love, far from being an antidote to powerlessness, is an expression of her power; it springs from her ability to see in the dark. This is a power just as real as the dazzling power of death.

When Psyche opens the box from Persephone, after emerging from the underworld into the light of day, what is suggested are the different requirements for living soulfully that obtain on the day-side of one's life as opposed to the night or dark-side. In the underworld, it was vital for Psyche to reflect on her soul, not only to exercise her power of knowing and loving, but to realize that she was engaged in knowing and loving, for that awareness of her own power kept her from succumbing to the fascinating power of death. The sleep that overtakes Psyche seems to symbolize forgetfulness. If it had overtaken her in the underworld, she would have been lost, for to be oblivious of her power there, even if she had continued to exercise it, would have left her vulnerable to death's fascination. Self-knowledge, implying self-consciousness of one's power of soul, is an absolute requirement for a fruitful experience of the dark side of one's life. But once back in the daylight world—the world of human relationships—self-consciousness is an obstacle to relating to others. When I am self-conscious, the other only reflects myself, but if this is the case, how can I find the divine spark in the other that will elicit my love? Psyche's interest is in loving, even more than in knowing. For her, knowing, that is, the self-knowledge that is awareness of the divine spark in oneself, could never be the end of her trials, but only a new kind of loving made possible by her soul's ability to see in the dark. That ability was potential in Psyche before she entered the underworld. Facing death relying on the divine spark that she couldn't see actualized that potential. But now, to love others, she must lose consciousness of that power.

It is like playing the piano. When you are learning a piece, you have to be aware of your technique—your fingering, hitting the right keys, keeping time—but once the piece is mastered, you can forget about technique and let the music take over.

The music of love, it turns out, has bright and dark themes: there are soaring moments, when the divine spark in my beloved kindles a blaze in me and then there are painful times when my love for the other is like a wound because the divine spark in him is in eclipse. What is essential to sustain my love during the painful times is the awareness that loving in the dark, loving amidst the ruin of all my dreams, is an expression of my innate power. Without this awareness, I could be destroyed—I could lose my will to live—should my lover's fire grow cold. If Rogozhin had discovered the divine spark within himself, he could have sustained the kind of painful love for Nastasya Filippovna that Prince Myshkin feels for her. Instead, his love for her becomes, as the Prince says, no different from hate and for the ruin he believes she has made of his life, he kills her and goes crazy. For Rogozhin, turning his back on Nastasya Filippovna and trying to make something of his life altogether different from what he had with her was not a real option. Rogozhin is a lover and his tribe either learns the secret of enduring love or destroys themselves. In the myth, when Zeus declares that the love of Eros and Psyche will last forever, he is implicitly praising Psyche for discovering the secret of enduring love. The power this represents is conveyed by her becoming a goddess.

The happy ending of Eros and Psyche is much more profound than any promise that they will live "happily ever after." I think of happiness as excluding pain, whereas the enduring love that will characterize the marriage of Eros and Psyche encompasses pain—the pain of loving in the dark, loving when there is an eclipse of the light in the beloved and he seems utterly distant. If it is "the deep magic from the dawn of time"—which we have associated with the power of death and its fascination for us—which causes an eclipse of the light, then we can associate enduring love, which is not extinguished by death, with "the deeper magic from before the dawn of time," of which C. S. Lewis also speaks.[40] The lion-king Aslan comes back to life in virtue of this "deeper magic" and so our souls catch fire again, we can love the other freely and passionately on his return—instead of being stuck in the fear and despair stirred up in our souls by death. The reunion with the beloved, which we experience as sheer sensual delight (the significance, it seems, of Psyche's giving birth to Pleasure), is the same and yet different from the initial encounter with him. We are enraptured, once again, by beauty, but this time we can let it nourish us and are not driven by it to attempt to possess the other. Beauty, it seems, is the original sacrament. It participates in that "deeper magic from before the dawn of time" that can break the spell of death, if only we let it.

What if my lover never returns? Once we have integrated the power of soul, it can catch fire nonetheless—and this is the miracle, not that the lover returns, but that, having passed through death, we can come back to life—to the fullness of life that a passionate existence implies. To have integrated soul means that we are vulnerable—that the heart is pierced—by every appearance of beauty: beauty in women as well as in men, beauty in children, beauty in plants and trees and cloudless skies. The appearance of beauty puts a great ache in the one who has integrated soul and when we consent to ache, to ache forever, if need be, the soul catches fire. The underworld journey, when it is made in the spirit in which Psyche makes it—with an open, willing heart—enables a person to ache in the presence of beauty "forever." Previously, I would have lunged at the beautiful person or thing, but now, my knowledge of the divine spark enables me to experience a passion that is non-possessive, that grows stronger the more I simply look at the other. What a wonder, it seems, to be able to meet the other's gaze, instead of closing my eyes in a rapture of submission; how amazing, that I can relate to the other person to person. As I gaze on the other, it is the radiance of the other's personhood that holds me, but as the other returns my gaze, I can feel my own radiance.

There is a knowledge of self, it seems from the experience of meeting the other's gaze, that goes beyond self-consciousness. Self-consciousness is knowledge of self through reflection. In this case, I know myself by thinking about myself. The self-knowledge made possible by the loving gaze of the other, however, we could call self-knowledge through participation. In this case, I know myself by being myself, by giving expression to the divine spark that dwells in, but is not limited to, me. Because it is not limited to me, I have to say that I participate in the divine spark, in the mystery of personhood, and I can go on to say that through that participation I am linked, in a fundamental way, to the other. In Psyche's journey, then, we can note three stages: first, when she is in the enchanted castle unaware of the divine spark within herself; second, when she is going through the trials culminating in the underworld journey, during which she derives power from her growing awareness of the divine spark; third, when she is reunited with Eros and participates in the divine spark through relationship with him. What is striking is that her journey does not end in knowing, but in loving or in the knowing that comes from loving where she knows herself in and through her relationship with the other and self-consciousness has been left behind.

Self-consciousness is never left behind completely, of course. My ecstatic participation with the other is something that comes and goes; when it is gone, the other and I are simply two people walking side by side. If the two of us have made a commitment to each other, then we share a common life, but the bonds that link us to that are of a different order than our ecstatic love. Focused on our common life, I have an earthbound sense of the other. Much of the time, I am preoccupied with the meeting of needs and am more like the washer women of James Joyce's *Finnegans Wake*[41] than a woman in love. The washer women, toiling ceaselessly on the banks of the River

Liffey, are depicted by Joyce as impersonal, like trees or rocks more than human beings. There is a danger that the spark of personhood, which flashes so brilliantly in loving exchanges, will be eclipsed by the unremitting cares of the common life. Love's ecstasy is a taste of heaven, while through the common life, we are rooted to the here and now. The person who has integrated soul, however, can never be just a washer woman. With a thousand duties pressing on her and her lover out of reach, she knows to fan the fire within by acts of loving attention. By believing in the divine spark—in herself and in those around her—she effects a release of its energy into the human circle.

The myths we have considered—"Inanna's Descent," *The Hymn to Demeter*, and *Amor and Psyche*—when taken in sequence, as we have done, seem to comprise a single story. We could call it, the story of an angry woman learning to love. The story begins in the dark heart of Inanna's anger, proceeds to Demeter's discovery of the power of spirit, and culminates in Psyche's ensoulment. Speaking your heart—even if it is filled with rage—seems to be the message of the first myth and being in touch with her heart—"having a care," as we put it— is what makes Demeter Demeter in the second myth we interpreted. If you don't have a care, according to the second myth, you'll never come to the point of making a commitment and the struggle for wholeness which ensues from that. The turning point in that struggle, we saw, is the acceptance of death, for this act of relenting reveals the power of spirit— our infinite capacity to relate to what happens to us, instead of becoming the victim of what happens. From the standpoint of spirit, I can embrace all the different aspects of myself— specifically, the maid, the mother, and the crone—and become whole. Psyche's journey, in turn, presupposes wholeness for without it the divine spark at the center of herself would be obscured by conflict. In her story, the divine spark becomes a fire that sustains her in and through her experience of the power of death.

The journey we have described is also a progression from an undifferentiated experience of impersonal powers to a realization of one's innate, personal power. When Inanna flies into a rage over Dumuzi's indifference, she is surrendering to the impersonal power of death—for Dumuzi's indifference is a taste of death. She is letting it close her mind and harden her heart until she becomes the death-dealing Ereshkigal who is blind to the spark of personhood in herself as well as in others. It is only through the sympathy of Enki's creatures, we saw, that the spark of personhood in the hag-queen is revived. Demeter's story hinges on the personal exchange that takes place between a human being and the Living God when the power of death, recognized as the destroying arm of God, is assented to. There is a moment when the mystery of God is penetrated, when dread gives way to exaltation and one knows, if only implicitly, that one's personhood is grounded in God. In Psyche's story, the threat to personhood comes primarily from the impersonal force of the instincts. Through the tasks she accomplishes, Psyche succeeds in differentiating the divine spark of her personhood—her ability to know and love—from the blind tendencies of her instincts. In the culminating task, her journey through the underworld, the personal power of love triumphs over the most intractable of our instincts—the tendency to resist an experience of death.

We cannot leave our study of ancient myths depicting women's experience without feeling, as modern women, a certain nostalgia. All the stories we interpreted have happy endings—even Inanna's story insofar as she claims the dark heart of her anger and does not get stuck in depression and self-hatred. For all their difficulties, these ancient protagonists seem to be propelled forward by a certain instinct for life. The hag-queen reaches out to receive the sympathy of Enki's creatures instead of remaining in her self-destructive isolation. Demeter becomes willing to live the life that is given her instead of persisting in her attitude of refusal. And Psyche—naive little Psyche—trusts that the flame of love in her will not be extinguished by the power of death. Modern women's stories do not always have a happy ending. That essential link to the life-force, which enables a woman to grow and change as life changes on her, seems to be missing from these accounts. What is blocking this vital connection in women's lives today? What would be required for its recovery? By comparing stories which exhibit this broken connection with modern women's stories which have a happy ending or fruitful outcome, we should be able to determine the shape of the modern woman's journey.

THREE

The Child and the Hag: Sylvia Plath

What does the heart want? Any woman brave enough to explore this question stands in the tradition of Inanna, Demeter, and Psyche. In *Portrait of the Artist as a Young Man*, Stephen Daedalus writes that his mother, on the eve of his departure from Ireland, is praying that "away from home and friends" he will "learn . . . what the heart is and what it feels."[1] What is striking is the idea that we leave home to know our hearts. This seems to conflict with the saying "Home is where the heart is," until we realize that having a heart—and therefore, a place that we call home—and knowing the heart are two different things. If having a heart is part and parcel of being human, knowing the heart is the individual's destiny. We take up this task in response to a call that differentiates us once and for all from the group, the particular neighborhood of the human circle into which we were born. But to respond to the call is to act for all humanity. "Welcome, O life!" Stephen writes. "I go to encounter for the millionth time the reality of experience and to forge in the smithy of my soul the uncreated conscience of my race."[2] The depths of heart the individual plumbs resonate universally. Whereas Stephen's mother was praying for him to succeed on the journey, the twentieth century has seen more and more women who are making the journey themselves.

How do you recognize a call to your heart? It would be nice if it were as clear as birdsong, but the modern woman's initiation into the mysteries of Inanna, Demeter, and Psyche is inevitably obscure. It is not that we lack those occasions which make "the hair rise and the heart leap," as Robert Graves puts it,[3] but rather, that we lack the frame of reference that would allow us to appreciate their value. Marija Gimbutas says that the wave of invasion which began the destruction of the Goddess-centered civilization in Old Europe was spearheaded by people on horseback who worshiped the "God of the shining sky."[4] As sky gods and solar symbolism became dominant, the significance of the underworld journey decreased. The shinning sky is dazzling. Compared to it, darkness is other, fearful. A devotee of the shining sky regards as temptation the yearnings awakened by night and the moon. It takes more than courage for such a person to follow those yearnings into the underworld and back. It was difficult enough, we must assume, in the times of Inanna, Demeter, and Psyche, when goddess religion or "women's mysteries" was a viable, if subordinate, religious option. In our time, when God the Father, who is simply a sky god for many Christians, has reigned exclusively for centuries, our longing for the dark is apt to be repressed. Our only connection to goddess religion may be the sense of a lack, of a dead space, in our lives and relationships. The first step of the journey in our time may be to recognize our lack.

The problem is compounded for those women in our culture who feel the dominance of the Christian sky god as a direct influence in the power wielded by the father or father-figures in their lives. As little girls—and I was one—these women were enthralled by their fathers. My father seemed all-powerful and all-knowing. If he was also remote and inaccessible that seemed only appropriate, for why should such an exalted being ever give me his attention? There were other influences in my formative years—a nature-loving grandmother, in particular—

but my primary identity was that of my father's daughter. My devotion to him was both conscious and unconscious; consciously, I strove to win his approval in everything I did and said; unconsciously, I mirrored his feelings. Looking back, I can see that I felt a lack in this worship of my father. I was drawn to boys who were dark and dreamy, who made the light of my father seem harsh. But I could never justify my attraction to them. So I always put them aside, eventually, and took up a new project. I am now middle-aged. The lack I felt as a child has become the split between two opposing selves: "Sarah Sanguine" or the dutiful daughter and a deeply buried woman. What I want is a way to resolve the split. I want an integral vision for my life and relationships. I want a new religion.

In resolving the split between a dutiful daughter persona and a deeply buried woman which I—and many twentieth-century women—experience, everything depends on how we identify the deeply buried woman. Intuitively, I have connected her with the goddess tradition. Here is the text of a poem I wrote in which these figures first appeared:

An Invocation

O deeply buried woman, come forth!
I know you not but I know you are there.
You are straining at my womb,
Pressing against the opening,
Struggling to intrude on the topside of my life.

Sarah Sanguine doesn't want you.
She is a murderess.
She commits abortions daily,
Teasing and laughing.
A light-hearted murderess she
And unrepentant.

But I want you, woman of darkness,
Daughter of Silence, I love you.
For me, the travail is sweet,
The hour of parturition longed for.

Sarah sparkles, but your darkness is holy.
She sings, but your silence is deep.
She looks and sighs and swoons and cries
But cannot love.
She clutches people like shiny objects,
Then casts them away.
(She doesn't mean to kill you, woman of darkness.
She'd be ever so sorry if she knew
And ask God and the angels and saints to forgive her—)
    Poor Sarah!
She lives by dreaming
And loves by touching
And all she has
Are happily ever after hopes
And half-remembered kisses.

In her weariness, come forth.
As her chatter dies away, be born.

Nearly twenty years have passed since I wrote this poem. I am ready to know the deeply buried woman.

Much of the twentieth-century women's literature portrays the situation in which a woman's everyday life is split off from that of a deeply buried woman inside her. One thinks of Edna, in Kate Chopin's book *The Awakening*, whose life was comfortable but monotonous until she taps a source of great freedom and power in herself during a moonlit swim.[5] Or of the protagonist in Margaret Atwood's *Surfacing*, who lives life as a victim until she sheds her social identity and goes wild in the Canadian North.[6] Then there is Sylvia Plath, whose novel entitled *The Bell Jar*, which is based on Plath's own experience, portrays the breakdown of a young woman whose identity depends solely on external achievement.[7] We deny the dark woman to our peril, it seems. But who is there among us who can conjure her up? Conjuring is an art not easily learned by women in our culture who are more like Plath's heroine than we like to admit. We have been taught that the power of a resolute will can accomplish anything. We have a hard time believing that what our fixed will and effort cannot

achieve is important. Yet the goddess tradition has its adher-
ents, even in out time. Sylvia Plath, Virginia Woolf, and Etty
Hillesum are master conjurers. Let us turn to Plath, first of
all as someone who conjures up the primitive aspect of the
"deeply buried woman."

THE CHILD FACING THE HAG

The appeal of Sylvia Plath for a woman who feels that
half of herself is buried is the recognition, in Plath's life and
work, of a similar split. In "Two Sisters of Persephone," a
poem Plath wrote in 1956 (the year of her marriage to Ted
Hughes), she expresses the division between an outer woman
and an inner woman:

> Two girls there are:
> within the house
> One sits; the other, without
> Daylong a duet of shade and light
> Plays between these.[8]

In *A Closer Look at Ariel*, Nancy Hunter Steiner's memoir of
Plath, the author comments on the difference between the
image of Plath conveyed and what Steiner knew about her.
Recalling her impression of Plath as a student at Smith the se-
mester following her suicide attempt and subsequent hospitali-
zation, Steiner writes, "except for the penetrating intelligence
and the extraordinary poetic talent, she could have been an
airline stewardess or the ingenuous heroine of a B movie. She
did not appear tortured or alienated; at times, it was difficult
for me to believe that she had ever had a self-destructive impulse."[9] Reading the poem in light of Steiner's memoir, it is
easy to associate the "ingenuous heroine" with the girl who sits
outside the house and the unobserved self-destructive impulses with the girl within. More than most women, Sylvia
Plath was unaware of the dark woman inside her. Finding her
voice as an artist meant letting the dark woman speak.

As early as 1956, as the title "Two Sisters of Persephone" indicates, Plath was using the imagery of the goddess tradition to express her experience of duality. In *Chapters in a Mythology*,[10] Judith Kroll demonstrates the influence on Plath's work of Robert Graves's epic, *The White Goddess*. This massive testimony to the pervasive power of goddess religion in ancient cultures was embraced by Plath, Ted Hughes says, because she felt "it gave shape to what had happened to her."[11] In the descent of the goddess to the underworld, she could see her own suicide attempt and period of extreme depression. In her relationship with her father—the "God" of her childhood who died when she was eight[12]—she could see the goddess's passionate attachment to her consort, who also descends to the underworld. The contrasting images of "Two Sisters of Persephone" remind us of the antithetical pair Inanna-Ereshkigal. The girl outside the house is "Bronzed as earth." On a "green altar / Freely become sun's bride . . . [she] Grows quick with seed." The other, the girl within, is "bitter / And sallow as any lemon," with "rat-shrewd . . . squint eyes." "[W]ry virgin to the last / [she] Goes graveward with flesh laid waste / Worm-husbanded, yet no woman."[13] In the ancient story of Inanna's descent, the goddess and the hag-queen alternate as phases in a woman's life. In Plath's poem, they inhabit her consciousness simultaneously.

When the woman within is the hag-queen, the quest for self-knowledge can seem dangerous. All her rage at loss and death, one knows instinctively, threatens the super-structure of normal life. The natural tendency is to turn outward, away from the simmering volcano, but the fascination of the hag is relentless. A fine thing for a woman just married to be writing about the hag! Sylvia Plath also wrote about her husband—as a kind of nature deity—during this period. In "Ode for Ted," she portrays him as a consort worthy of the goddess:

> For his least look, scant acres yield:
> each finger-furrowed field
> heaves forth stalk, leaf, fruit-nubbed emerald;[14]

Sexuality and death as opposing yet complementary powers is a recurring theme in these poems written around the time of her marriage. Young girls and their lovers are juxtaposed with witches and crone-figures. In William Broyles's essay, "Why Men Love War,"[15] he remembers from his first Vietnam experience how the imminence of death for soldiers makes sex more intense. With Plath, the accent falls more frequently on death. In poem after poem, the depiction of sexual love serves to underscore the awfulness of our mortality. "Crystal Gazer," a poem from late 1956, moves abruptly from a fortune teller's prediction of marital happiness for a young couple to her vision of a death's head.[16]

Unlike the ancients, we moderns have no rituals for enacting our relationship to sexuality and death. Through the sacred marriage rite, when the king had intercourse with the high-priestess—the representative of the goddess—we have to imagine that the whole community, who usually participated in their own acts of love-making at this time, had a powerful experience of the life-force. Similarly when the king "joined the goddess of the underworld," i.e., when he died or was killed or his death simulated, they must have had a vicarious experience of the power of death.[17] This regular enactment of ritual sexuality and ritual death taught the people, we can assume, the alternation of these powers in a human life: a period of thriving and prospering giving way to a period of loss and withdrawal, followed by another upsurge of the life-force and a continuation of the cycle. Poems for 1956 suggest that Plath was trying to strike a ritual balance between death and sexuality through her art, but "The Lady and the Earthenware Head"[18] from 1957 indicates that her consciousness was really dominated by the hag. In the poem, a woman is trying to rid herself of a ceramic head in her likeness. Repelled by its "spite-set / Ape of her look," she wants to get it out of her sight while feeling "loath to junk it." She considers removing it to a trash heap, a marsh, and a willow grove, but the fascination of the head is paralyzing. In the end, "Despite her wrung hands, her tears, her praying 'Vanish!'" it remains "shrined on her shelf . . .og[ling] her" with "its basilisk look of love."

By the time she was writing her mature poetry, Sylvia Plath's actual experience of the power of death had been significant. When the father she idolized died when she was eight, she told her mother, "I'll never speak to God again"[19] and then seems to have cut herself off from her feelings:

> The day you died I went into the dirt,
> Into the lightless hibernaculum
> Where bees, striped black and gold, sleep out the blizzard
> Like hieratic stones, and the ground is hard.[20]

"Electra on Azalea Path," written in 1959, describes the long "wintering" of a traumatized soul. It conveys the sense of soulless existence as a kind of half-life, where "Everything [takes] place in a durable whiteness" and events have the flattened-out quality of dream images. Her next encounter with death seems to have been her visit to her father's grave when she was twenty. *The Bell Jar*, her autobiographical novel, places the visit before her suicide attempt:

> Then I remembered that I had never cried for my father's death. . . . I laid my face to the smooth face of the marble and howled my loss into the cold salt rain.[21]

"Electra on Azalea Path" describes this moment as an awakening: "The day I woke, I awoke on Churchyard Hill." Plath was flooded, apparently, with all the emotions surrounding her father's death that she had repressed. But the awakening to her dark side almost destroyed her. For months after she tried to kill herself, Plath was depressed. She was so unfocused that she couldn't read. "Blank and stopped as a dead baby"[22] is how Esther, the protagonist of *The Bell Jar*, describes herself in the hospital. Plath's therapy included a series of shock treatments.

Although Plath refers in *The Bell Jar* to the protagonist's release from the asylum as a kind of rebirth, it is clear from the way she portrays it that it is only partial. Attending the funeral of a friend from the hospital who finally succeeded in committing suicide, Esther feels an upsurge of the life-force: "I took a deep breath and listened to the old brag of my heart, I am, I am, I am."[23] But in the next scene, as Esther is waiting for her exit interview, feeling "scared to death," she reflects, "There ought to be a ritual for being born twice—patched, retreaded, and approved for the road."[24] Further indication that Esther's rebirth is ungoddess-like is the way she approaches the panel of doctors. Like a timid child, instead of relying on her own power, she takes her cue from the expectations of others: "The eyes and faces all turn themselves toward me and guiding myself by them as by a magical thread, I stepped into the room."[25] When a return from the underworld is incomplete, when the upsurge of the life-force is inhibited, one inhabits the land of the living as a kind of alien. However involved the person is in work and relationship, part of her is always withdrawn, gazing toward the land of the dead. Esther's mother tells her that they are going to take up where Esther left off before her breakdown and act as if it were all "a bad dream." But Esther knows she will never forget "the cadavers . . . Doctor Gordon's wall-eyed nurse, the twenty pounds she gained on insulin and the rock that bulged between sky and sea like a gray skull . . . they were part of me," is how she puts it, "They were my landscape."[26]

The incompleteness of her return from the underworld is reflected in the "I" of much of Plath's poetry before 1961. The timid child we see in Esther at the end of *The Bell Jar* is the speaker of these poems. There is an alternation between the child's fascination with death, coupled with her longing for the father whom she has lost, and her dread of death symbolized by her struggles with the hag-queen. "Full Fathom Five" evokes the way the idolized dead can continue to enthrall us, casting their magnetism beyond the grave so that we are almost as enchanted as when they were alive:

You defy other godhood.
I walk dry on your kingdom's border
Exiled to no good.

Your shelled bed I remember.
Father, this thick air is murderous.
I would breathe water.[27]

"The Disquieting Muses" reminds me of a series of dreams I had when I was in my twenties in which a small child in shining white is searching room after room of her house looking for her mother. Finally, in one room, she finds a woman in bed who is not her mother, but a hideous slattern, who rises up to give the child a smothering embrace. Plath's poem, inspired by a de Chirico painting with the same title, expresses the feeling of abandonment of a child whose mother cannot protect her from the three "Mouthless, eyeless . . . baldhead[ed]" ladies who are her constant companions. While her mother floats "in bluest air . . . with / Flowers and blue-birds that never were / Never, never found anywhere," the child is left on the ground to face her companions.[28]

A child confronting the hag—this is the theme of how many fairy tales? The pristine and the primordial, innocence and power—not united but split so that innocence is weak and power is ugly. A woman experiencing this kind of split is not really relating to death but to her rage against death cut off from her ego because unclaimed by her. The baleful sisters of Plath's poem convey the moment just prior to rage, when it is still terror, the cold fear in the pit of your stomach. A woman's return from the underworld is incomplete, it seems, when she fails to claim the power of the hag, when she fails to appropriate her fear and rage at death. If we think of the encounter with death as a kind of initiation ritual from which the mature man or woman is meant to emerge, then what makes it effective would be the willingness of the person to take into herself the knowledge of death. The dominance of the child-figure, on the contrary, symbolized the persistence of denial, the willful refusal to let one's spirit be tempered by the fact of death. In "Tale of a Tub," a partly whimsical poem from 1956, Plath contrasts the child's eye view of the world, which peoples it with fabulous creatures, with the sober perception of reality. Interestingly, it is the fabulous realm which she finds reassuring; the "poverty" of the "merely actual," she declares, "assaults [the] ego." Our differentiation from the world, which makes possible an objective perception of it, appears to her as a fall from grace:

> Just how guilty are we when the ceiling reveals no cracks that can be decoded? When washbowl maintains it has no more holy calling than physical ablution and the towel dryly disclaims that fierce troll faces lurk in its explicit folds?[29]

The formula of fairy tales dictates a happy ending: the child always escapes from the hag. But since there is no real confrontation with death, only with the specter of the fear of death, the child is unchanged and will be waylaid by the hag, we know, another day. Since she never becomes the hag, the way Inanna dies as the goddess and metamorphoses into Ereshkigal, the child never loses her innocence the way the goddess does. It is precisely the fairytale mentality that Plath celebrates in "Tale of a Tub." The undazzled eye, she thinks, discloses a bleak and even revolting vista. "Absolute fact," the in-itselfness of the world, those "intransigent lines" that our dreams can never wholly blur she rejects. The remedy is to imitate the imaginative mode of the child:

> . . . accuracy must not stalk at large:
> each day demands we create our whole world over,
> disguising the constant horror in a coat
> of many-colored fictions; we mask our past
> in the green of eden, pretend future's shining fruit
> can sprout from the navel of this present waste.

What the child in her innocence takes for truth—the correspondence of the world to the way she imagines it to be—Plath presents as clearly false. But the "usual terror" of our ordinary existence demands, she thinks, that we choose the realm of fantasy over real life. Enthrallment is preferable, apparently, to the despair that underlies the perception of existence as empty. Despair, however, is way below the surface in this poem. Announcing her project of turning the truth of her experience into something fantastic, Plath is gaily defiant:

> . . . in faith
> we shall board our imagined ship and wildly sail
> among sacred islands of the mad 'till death
> shatters the fabulous stars and makes us real.

If the mythic mode represents a tapping of the power of instinct—our instinct for life in the face of death—the fairytale mode corresponds to the repression of instinct. Instead of working through her fear and rage at death in the asylum, Plath seems to have re-buried it, but images of death kept coming to the surface. Some of her best poems before 1961 evoke a ceaseless brooding on these images. "It is no night to drown in," the speaker declares at the beginning of "Lorelei."[30] She stands firmly on shore "in a well-steered country, / Under a balanced ruler." But the depths work their fascination on her:

> . . . these shapes float
> Up toward me, troubling the face
> Of quiet . . .
>
> . . . They sing
> Of a world more full and clear
> Than can be . . .

The speaker resists: "You lodge on the pitched reefs of nightmare," she tells the Lorelei and decries their "ice-hearted calling." But under the river's spell, she eventually sees the shapes as "goddesses of peace" and prays, "Stone, stone, ferry me down there." In "Full Fathom Five," there is the same initial resistance to the white-haired, white-bearded man who washes in with the sea and the same concluding acknowledgment of the desire he evokes in her.[31]

When living out a denial of death, a person is very susceptible to the allure of death. Knowledge of death and the dark side completes us as human beings; if we deny death on one level, on a deeper level, we will crave that knowledge. Anne Sexton wrote a memoir of Plath in which she recounts late afternoons over cocktails at the Ritz when she and Plath would describe to each other their suicide attempts. "We talked death with burned up intensity, both of us drawn to it like moths to an electric light bulb."[32] In "Wanting to Die," the poem Sexton wrote with Plath's ultimate suicide in mind, she refers to "the almost unnamable lust."[33] The great danger, when living out a denial of death, is that a brush with death will expose that desire and leave you vulnerable to it. This is what happens to Susan Rawlings, the protagonist of Doris Lessing's story, "To Room 19." By middle age she has put together the perfect life for herself: marriage to a successful lawyer, four beautiful children, and a house in the suburbs. But clearly, something is missing. One day in the garden she encounters the figure of Death and after that her life is a series of withdrawals. First, she leaves her family to spend time in her room. Next, she leaves her house once a week to sit in a cheap hotel room in London. Finally, she leaves her body—opening up the gas jets in the room and lying down on the bed. "She was quite content lying there, listening to the faint soft hiss of the gas . . . as she drifted off into the dark river."[34]

To keep from being seduced by death, we have to meet it with our instinct for life. The encounter with death has to be a confrontation. A woman is like Susan Rawlings, passive in the face of death, when her desire for knowledge of death and the dark side eclipses her desire for life. The ascendancy of that desire blinds her to her heart's connection to all the things of her life: her home, her husband, her children. At the age of twenty-six, when Plath and Anne Sexton were regularly discussing death over cocktails, Plath's heart would seem to have been engaged in the life of her husband, Ted Hughes. Her love for him would appear to have been the center of the life she was creating for herself. "My whole thought is how to please him," she wrote her mother. "The joy of being a loved and loving woman, that is my song."[35] Yet when we compare Plath's poetry with her letters home from this period, it is clear that her life was running on two separate tracks. On the surface, it reflected her dreams of marriage and a brilliant career; beneath the surface, her obsession with death threatened to sabotage those dreams. "A Life," written in 1960, the year her first child was born, contrasts a "family, / Of valentine faces . . . Every one of them permanently busy" with a "woman dragging her shadow in a circle / About a bald hospital saucer." She likens the saucer to the moon—a symbol associated with the hag—and indicates the utter stasis of the woman's life. "She lives quietly / With no attachments, like a foetus in a bottle." However genuine Plath's love for her husband, it was not, it seems, her only "song." Her soul was mesmerized by the image of her dead father: "The future is a gray seagull . . . And a drowned man, complaining of the great cold / Crawls up out of the sea."[36]

THE CHILD OVERTAKEN BY THE HAG

The hag who is close to the surface in Plath's pre-1961 poems breaks through in a poem Plath wrote from a hospital bed early that year. After seeing her image over and over, we recognize the hag's voice immediately. It is spiteful—in sharp contrast to the sweetness of Plath's child persona. The hag appears alongside the child—who is portrayed as a plaster "saint"—trapped in their unhappy "marriage." "In Plaster" is the hag's complaint against the child:

I shall never get out of this! There are two of me now.
This new absolutely white person and the old yellow one.
And the white person is certainly the superior one.
She doesn't need food, she is one of the real saints.
At the beginning I hated her, she had no personality—
She lay in bed with me like a dead body.[37]

"Old yellow" (as one critic calls her[38]) resents the plaster saint for her illusion of superiority. Having been grateful to "old yellow," at first, for giving her a soul, the saint has become "offish." She is critical of "old yellow" for "[having kept] her in the dark" and wants to end the relationship. The real problem, the hag says, is that the "saint" "thought she was immortal" and was tired of "Wasting her days waiting on a half-corpse." So the hag is plotting her revenge:

> Now I see that it must be one or the other of us.
> She may be a saint and I may be ugly and hairy
> But she'll soon find out that that doesn't matter a bit.
> I'm collecting my strength; one day I shall manage
>   without her.

What does it mean for the hag to eclipse the child in oneself? If the dominance of the child represents the repression of instinct—denial in the face of death and the dark side—her being overtaken by the hag would signal the release of instinct as a dark force in one's life. Our desire for life in the face of death is our deepest, darkest desire. But this first appearance of the hag seems to have been too much for Plath. In the very next poem she wrote after "In Plaster," it is the child's voice we hear again expressing the kind of fascination with death that makes us experience our desire for life as painful. "The tulips are too excitable, it is winter here," Plath writes, from the same hospital bed from which she wrote "In Plaster."[39] In "Tulips," the speaker is experiencing a bouquet of tulips as a kind of assault. "I didn't want any flowers," she protests, "I only wanted / To lie with my hands turned up and be utterly empty." The tulips "concentrate her attention," while she prefers being left unfocused. Her husband and child smile at her from the family photo, but all she feels are "little smiling hooks" catching onto her skin. Instead of identifying with her beating heart, she likens it to the intrusive tulips: "it opens and closes its bowl of red blooms" keeping her on the side of life. But she is dreaming of the other side, tasting water that is "warm and salt, like the sea" coming from "a country far away as health."

Why would a woman resist the emergence of her hag? Feeling the power of her awesome desire for life, why would she retreat to the standpoint of denial? It can only be because she has failed to recognize the hag as the goddess; she has failed to see the power of life, of her desire for life, in the hag's rage. Judith Kroll argues that the presence of the moon goddess or hag in Plath's late poems indicates that they are about rebirth.[40] But this interpretation fails to recognize the despair with which Plath relates to the hag in her late poems. Rage and grief are a prelude to rebirth when one says yes to rage and grief, when one trusts that one will come through the dark time. This is the trust Inanna has when she undertakes her underworld journey. Reading "The Descent," we are never for a minute in doubt of her return from the underworld. Her preparations for the journey signify an ordeal to be endured. The contrast between Inanna's attitude toward the hag— whom she calls "my sister"—and Plath's is striking. Plath identifies with the hag in her late poems, but it is an identification that seems to have been born of necessity and hence, is alternatingly resigned and defiant. When someone is not ready for the underworld journey, when she identifies with her hag despairingly, the results can be catastrophic. Plath's late poems exhibit a woman trapped in her grief and rage against death.

Seven months after the two poems written from Plath's hospital bed, in which the hag-figure and the child seem to be at odds with each other, Plath wrote "The Moon and the Yew Tree" which is remarkable for its clarity about the author's identification with the hag. Reading this poem, we sense that Plath has crossed a line: having portrayed the hag, having spoken in her voice, she now claims the hag's dark landscape as her own:

> This is the light of the mind, cold and planetary.
> The trees of the mind are black. The light is blue.
> The grasses unload their griefs on my feet as if I were God,

> Pricking my ankles and murmuring of their humility.
> Fumy, spirituous mists inhabit this place.[41]

The speaker is standing in a churchyard "Separated from [her] house by a row of headstones." The yew tree in the church-yard points to the moon. As Judith Kroll demonstrates, the moon-muse is a central figure in Plath's late poems.[42] Here, she embraces her muse in the voice of someone acquiescing to her fate:

> The moon is my mother. She is not sweet like Mary.
> Her blue garments unloose small bats and owls.
> How I would like to believe in tenderness—
> The face of the effigy, gentled by candles
> Bending, on me in particular, its mild eyes.

The tone of lament in the poem bespeaks the regret in Plath's farewell to the pristine child's experience of life which is evoked by the references to Mary. Mary seems to represent for Plath that unconditional love that the child craves. The moon-mother, by contrast, described in the following stanza as "bald and wild," seems to gaze on her children with indifference.

Reading "The Moon and the Yew Tree" with "The Descent of Inanna" in mind, we are struck by the fact that whereas Inanna relates to the hag as an aspect of herself, Plath seems to think of the hag as her true self. The poem indicates an opposition between Plath's house and where she actually lives. From the churchyard she can see her house, but it might as well belong to someone else:

> The moon is no door. It is a face in its own right.
> White as a knuckle and terribly upset.
> It drags the sea after it like a dark crime; it is quiet
> With the O-gape of complete despair. I live here.

The disjunction, expressed in the poem, between the inside and the outside of the church suggests that there is no way back to the standpoint of the pristine child which Plath has abandoned:

I have fallen a long way. Clouds are flowering
Blue and mystical over the face of the stars.
Inside the church, the saints will be all blue,
Floating on their delicate feet over the cold pews,
Their hands and faces stiff with holiness.
The moon sees nothing of this. She is bald and wild.
And the message of the yew tree is blackness—
　　blackness and silence.

The possibility of rebirth or new life is explicitly rejected in this poem: "Twice on Sunday, the [church] bells startle the sky—/. . . affirming the Resurrection." But they are a part of the world to which Plath now finds herself alien. We shudder to read, "I simply cannot see where there is to get to."

What makes Plath identify with the hag as her true self? Why does she despair of ever returning to the child's standpoint, where one "believe[s] in tenderness"? To identify with the hag as your true self, the poem makes clear, is to resign yourself to the ascendancy of the dark forces in your personality. It is to accept as inevitable the takeover of the personality by long-buried rage. Plath's desire for knowledge of death and the dark side seems to have shipwrecked in the hag's rage. But why would a woman get stuck in her rage? Why would she think there was no way out of the dark place in her heart for which violence seems to be the only adequate expression? In "The Descent," Inanna can count on the aid of her grandfather Enki to bring her back from the underworld. It is the sympathy of Enki's creatures, when she is beside herself with rage and grief, that restores her desire for life. In the first years of their marriage, Plath's husband seems to have played many roles for her, including that of the wise Enki. Her journals describe him as giving her a "steady love," as wanting her "to fight [her] devils with the best weapons she could muster and to win."[43] But in October 1961, when Plath was writing "The Moon and the Yew Tree," she had met the woman for whom her husband would leave her a year later. I believe the poem reflects Plath's knowledge that she was losing her husband.

Nothing hurts the child in you like rejection by one on whom you have depended for love. Rejection extinguishes the child's faith that happily ever after dreams come true. If a woman has been living the split between the child and the hag, it can seem, at this juncture, that she is doomed to play the hag.

In Plath's case, the loss of her husband would have recapitulated the defining experience of her life—the loss of her father. Once again, she was being abandoned. When she had relived the experience of her father's death the first time—at the age of twenty—she had been able to emerge from the clinical depression that ensued by re-establishing her pattern of denial. Whatever dark forces were lurking below the surface in Plath's life after her institutionalization, the dominance of the pristine child-figure had enabled her to sustain her work and relationships. From "The Moon and the Yew Tree," we can see that denial was no longer possible for Plath at the time that she and her husband were becoming estranged. In the lonely figure of the hag are reenacted both the child's feeling of abandonment and the young woman's experience of isolation. By identifying with the hag, Plath is admitting her fundamental aloneness. The dreadfulness of death, the reason we deny it, is the way it divorces us from the human community, the way it leaves us utterly alone. This is the knowledge Plath had both feared and desired. This is the truth she had never faced up to but had never been able to suppress entirely. The hag-figure of our nightmares is the woman alone. The perception of the growing distance between herself and her husband seems to have convinced Plath that she would never be other than a woman alone.

Being alone in the aftermath of a relationship that you had thought would take away your sense of aloneness is different from being alone in the expectation of such a relationship. In the latter case, a woman can convince herself that she is no different from any girl who dreams of a true love; in the former, it seems as though her basic inadequacy as a woman has been exposed. Failing at intimacy makes you feel like a pariah, as if there were some essential ingredient of femininity that you were lacking.

> I have tried not to think too hard. I have tried to be natural
> I have tried to be blind in love, like other women[44]

Plath writes, just two months before explicit reference to estrangement from her husband appears in her poetry. "Three Women, A Poem for Three Voices" is set in a maternity ward. The second voice is that of a woman who has miscarried. Instead of finding consolation in the company of the other women, she feels like an outcast. In a passage that calls to mind the hag, she questions her identity:

> I see myself as a shadow, neither man nor woman,
> Neither a woman happy to be like a man, nor a man
> Blunt and flat enough to feel no lack. I feel a lack.

When a woman questions her feminine identity, she is not simply feeling the sting of her lover's rejection. She is questioning whether she will ever succeed at intimacy. "Is this my lover then," the second woman asks, "this death, this death?"

Most of Plath's late poems—those from the last year of her life—are written in the voice of the hag. They are marvelous in the way that they chart the terrain of the hag's emotions. Characteristic of Plath's hag—and unlike what we saw in Ereshkigal—is the note of utter aloneness that is struck in a few poems and seems to resonate throughout the others. Women's powerlessness vis-à-vis men, which is how we explained Ereshkigal's rage, seems a small matter compared to our ultimate powerlessness vis-à-vis death and the aloneness of death. Plath's predicament, in this light, seems far more serious than Inanna's. The aloneness of death corresponds to a place in the heart which no human being can enter. It makes the power of sympathy—which helped Inanna overcome her self-hatred and despair—seem unavailing. What is interesting is the way that the sense of our utter aloneness co-exists, in some women, with a childlike enjoyment of life in the human circle. I think of a friend of mine who lived an apparently idyllic life in the country with her husband, children, and assorted farm animals. Sitting in her kitchen one afternoon as she was taking bread out of the oven, I complained of being alone and lonely. Her oracular retort came straight from the hag: "Don't you realize? Everyone is lonely." Like Plath, a woman can reach the point where her sense of aloneness overwhelms her childlike faith that "everything will be all right." Several years after our conversation, I heard that my friend and her husband had divorced.

The predicament when the disintegration of a relationship leaves a person up against the aloneness of death is that, whether she looks toward the human circle or away from it, there is only darkness. When she feels the aloneness of death but is not involved in a relationship, the human circle seems bright and filled with promise—as if linking her life with another might save her from the power of death. Conversely, when a woman is embedded in the human circle, weighed down by the needs and demands of others, it is the life outside the human circle, the solitary life, that seems bright. The freedom of the solitary life, she thinks, would be her salvation. But when a person has experienced both the failure of relationships and the loneliness of a life without them, it can seem that there is no hope, that no salvation is possible. Subconsciously aware of her fundamental aloneness ever since the death of her father, Plath had always on some level stood outside the human circle putting her hopes, consequently, in "the perfect relationship." "Elm," written in April 1962, shows how the troubled state of her marriage left her in an intolerable situation. "Is it the sea you hear in me / Its dissatisfactions? / the elm tree asks. Or the voice of nothing that was your madness?"[45] And then, "Love is a shadow. How you lie and cry after it." In the usual poem of love and loss, the dominant tone is sadness. But sadness in this poem gives way to something darker and more disturbing:

I am inhabited by a cry
Nightly it flaps out
Looking with its hooks, for something to love.
I am terrified by this dark thing
That sleeps in me;
All day I feel its soft, feathery turnings, its malignity.

The frightening aspect of the cry that "flaps out" at night
"looking . . . for something to love" makes "Elm" reminiscent
of some lines written by Thomas Merton, the Trappist monk,
just after he ended his relationship with the young woman he
fell in love with near the end of his life. "I thought I was
slowly being torn in half. Then several times while I was recit-
ing the office, felt silent cries come slowly tearing and rending
their way up out of the very ground of my being. It was
awful . . . I got scared. There was nothing I could do with
these metaphysical howls."[46] What is frightening about the
cries that issue from a broken heart is the extreme vulnerability they express. If we let ourselves feel the pain to the full,
down to the level of our utter aloneness, it seems it will destroy us, that we will never be able to close the broken circle
of the self. In Plath's case, the pain of a broken relationship
had almost destroyed her once before: getting in touch with
her grief over her father's death when she was twenty-one was
what had led to her suicide attempt. It is not surprising, then,
that in "Elm," there is both pain and anger. Her "metaphysical
howl" is tinged with "malignity." When feeling utterly alone,
being angry over the failure of a relationship is an automatic
survival reflex. It protects you from the full force of the pain,
the full force of your aloneness.

Plath's husband, as we would expect, is the chief target
of the anger expressed in the late poems. But the anger is
muted in the poems written before she and Ted Hughes actually separated—in late September or early October 1962. In
many of these, Plath seems to be taking the measure of her
changed situation, like a newly arrived prisoner tracing the
contours of her cell.

> A gray wall now, clawed and bloody.
> Is there no way out of the mind? [47]

Relationship with another, giving oneself to another, is a reprieve from the prison of our fundamental aloneness. How many women get married with an intense feeling of relief—the sense of having escaped a dreaded fate and guilty because the love they feel for their husbands has an undercurrent of desperation? When the other is used as a shield against death this way, the attachment has the character of a death grip. If the feeling of love dies, what is left is the naked attachment. "Tight wires between us," Plath writes, "Pegs too deep to uproot."[48] Plath's husband's lover is also the object of Plath's anger. In "The Other," she appears as Inanna to Plath's hag:

> I have your head on my wall.
> Navel cords, blue red and lucent,
>
> Shriek from my belly like arrows and these I ride
> O moon-glow, o sick one.[49]

The poem makes a reference to the other woman's barrenness—"The stolen horses, the fornications / Circle a womb of marble." By this time, Plath had two children and she seems to want to assert her fecundity against the other's lack. But the hag is stronger than the mother in her. The poem ends in a display of violence:

> I scratch like a cat.
> The blood that runs is dark fruit.

There is a difference between being angry and unleashing pent-up rage. For a woman in the habit of suppressing her rage, unleashing it is liberating. There is the feeling of power that always attends the emergence of unconscious contents. There is the satisfaction of connecting with oneself on a level that was buried. Her husband's departure seems to have been the impetus for the full expression of Plath's rage. With him physically present, she could continue to hope that she might not be abandoned. Toward that end, she probably kept her anger under control. But once he was gone, there was no holding back. Plath's poems from October 1962 are blistering. What is striking is that everyone close to Plath, not just her husband but the father she adored and the mother she wrote to almost daily, comes under attack. Only her children are spared. In a series of poems written at the beginning of the month, her "Bee" poems, Plath anticipates her rebirth as a woman of power. From the wreckage of her marriage, she seems to think, a new and glittering Sylvia—the true Sylvia—will emerge. The poem "Stings" describes a man who was so sweet that a whole swarm of bees attached themselves to his face. "They thought death was worth it," Plath comments, "but I / Have a self to recover, a queen. Is she dead, is she sleeping? / Where has she been? With her lion-red body, her wings of glass?"[50] The rage of the October poems identifies this self as the hag-queen—it is the hag-queen's moment of glory.

THE HAG-QUEEN TRIUMPHANT

The rage against death and the aloneness of death that many women carry around in their psyches truly creates an underworld peopled by the projection of their rage. The figures under attack in Plath's "October poems" (actually, the amazing flow of creativity that produced twenty-six poems in October yielded twelve more in November and two at the beginning of December before it stopped abruptly) suffer the same distortions as the figures in nightmares: they have the features of other people, but they embody the dreamer's dark side. To walk through this gallery is to enter the private world of Plath's nightmare and to leave the world we have in common, where self and other exist as opposing realities. There is an infernal pleasure in withdrawing into a private world—in letting your fantasies take over whether they be bright or dark. It is the pleasure of being your own god—of experiencing no resistance to your exercise of power. In the world we have in common, your reality limits me. I may transgress those limits, but as long as I retain the human perspective, I experience my act as a transgression. In my private world, however, there is the delicious feeling of license.

The close proximity of death can cause people to withdraw into their private worlds. First-time soldiers, Simone Weil says, experience war as unreality: they retreat from an honest acknowledgment of the death they face into the illusion of themselves as invincible.[51] When Ted Hughes left her, Plath's retreat into the realm of the hag-queen must have been instinctive. Instead of trying to understand her rage, she used it to fill the void of her aloneness.

The intensity of the "October poems" signals the desperate need they were meeting for Plath. "They saved me,"[52] she commented and the act of giving expression to a private world when the world we have in common seems full of death does preserve a sense of self. "Suicide is the opposite of a poem,"[53] Anne Sexton says; in writing these poems, Plath was making a choice against suicide. It was a deliberate choice, because only a few months earlier, she had tried to kill herself by driving her car off the road.[54] It is possible to create, through your art and in your life, a self that is other than the person you really are. A timid person, naturally fearful and hesitant, can create a confident persona to mask her timidity. A dependent person, who needs to link with another to be able to live with our fundamental aloneness, can forge an independent persona. Plath, we know, was extremely dependent. The bonds she formed with her father, mother, and husband were intense. In the seven years of their marriage, Ted Hughes says, he and his wife were apart for only a few days.[55] The self of *Ariel*, the collection of poems drawn mostly from the forty poems that streamed out of her after her husband left, seems to be a self that was forged as an alternative to the heartbroken woman Plath really was.

The agony of the heartbroken Sylvia appears in "A Birthday Present," a poem Plath wrote on September 30, 1962.[56] It describes the torment of waiting for her husband to make his decision to leave her final. "If you only knew how the clouds were killing my days," the speaker complains. "To you they are only transparencies, clear air. / But my god, the clouds are like cotton. / Armies of them. They are carbon monoxide." When your attachment to another is like a death-grip and the relationship seems doomed, the continued presence of the other, as the reminder of betrayal, is like a knife-blade to your heart. Every contact you have with the other—stirring up memories of your former intimacy—reinforces your sense of isolation. "Is it impossible for you to let something go and have it go whole?" the speaker asks. "Must you stamp each piece in purple, / Must you kill what you can?" In this poem, the only alternative Plath envisions to her agony is death. It concludes with the speaker wishing for a knife that would "not carve, but enter / Pure and clean as the cry of a baby" so that "the universe [might] slide from [her] side." A poem written the very next day, however, seems to signal the strategy of forging an alternative self that Plath chose, at least for a while, in preference to suicide. "The Detective" is an eerie poem which describes a crime in which a woman who was a wife and the mother of two children was vaporized. At the scene of the crime, the only traces of the woman are emblems of the hag:

> We walk on air, Watson.
> There is only the moon embalmed in phosphorus.
> There is only a crow in a tree. Make notes.[57]

From the standpoint of her self of power, such a woman's life is an emergence from servitude. She loses her memory in the underworld of the love that inspired the tasks she performed. "Love Letter," a poem Plath wrote about her husband in 1960 begins "Not easy to state the change you made. / If I'm alive now, then I was dead."[58] But two years later, in "Stings," she portrays her life with him as bondage.

> I stand in a column
> Of winged, unmiraculous women,
> Honey drudgers.

> I am no drudge
> Though for years I have eaten dust
> And dried plates with my dense hair.[59]

The dependency that love creates is despised by the self of power. Marriage seems to have taken you "the way of all women"[60] leaving you undazzling and unremarkable. All the resentment Plath felt in her marriage—toward the restrictions of domesticity and her husband's self-centeredness—now fuels her pursuit of a glittering way of her own. Does every woman who is mired in domesticity dream of soaring above the relentless routine of needing and being needed so that her undomestic self, her wild self, can shine? When her husband leaves, the goddess he brought to life may be dead, but the hag remains. "Now she is flying," Plath exults, "More terrible than she ever was. . . ."[61]

If you could only let the hag fly free—the way some women do in their dreams—if you could only accept your solitary side, your wild side, it would not be "terrible." There are women who live outside the human circle who are fascinating—especially to other women. Think of Mademoiselle Reisz in Kate Chopin's novel, *The Awakening*. She is an entrancing presence on the sidelines of the heroine's life who steps forward to encourage Edna when she is about to leave her husband. She tells Edna that she must have strong wings to do what she is doing.[62] If a woman is angry at death and aloneness—if she hates her solitary side—her flight will be erratic. There will be moments—in nature, with a child—when time stands still and she seems to float: "Your clear eye is the one absolutely beautiful thing," Plath wrote in "Child"[63] just two weeks before she killed herself. But her anger hooks her to everyone she ever loved whom she thought would protect her from death and aloneness. In the angriest poems in *Ariel*, Plath is overtly announcing her independence from the people closest to her. She accuses them of having tyrannized and manipulated her. The irony is that it is she who is using them—now as dark figures—so as to continue to be shielded from death and aloneness. We should read the darkest poem, "Daddy" not just as Plath's way of releasing her pent-up rage toward the men in her life, but as a way of avoiding the fact of their absence.

When a woman has adored someone—made him the god of her life—there is a grinning dark god who is ready to replace him when the relationship suffers a break. Every woman who has ever been a devotee, molding herself to another's expectations, could write a poem like "Daddy" in which Plath portrays the central character in her personal mythology as a Nazi.[64] Someone who is a devotee has succumbed to the spell of another's power. A break with the other is an opportunity to become grounded in herself. But if she needs to be under a spell—if she is afraid or despairing of an existence in which she is not magically linked to the other—her hatred of him will be as passionate and enduring as her devotion. In "Tale of a Tub," we remember, Plath proclaimed her need to be mesmerized. In an earlier piece, "Ocean 1212-W," she laments the day when "[her] beautiful fusion with the things of this world was over" and she discovered "the *separateness* of everything."[65] Being in love—with father or with husband—can re-create the fusion with the world we all experienced as children. When a father dies or a husband leaves, hating him as the autocrat who enslaved you is a way of remaining fused to him. The feeling of power that comes from expressing this hatred is illusory. "Daddy, daddy, you bastard, I'm through," the poem ends, and we want Plath to sink down from her rage into her own authentic center. But it doesn't happen. When you play the hag defiantly, as Plath does, your rage is your center.

"Medusa" is ostensibly an attempt of Plath's to free herself from her mother. "In any case, you are always there, / Tremulous breath at the end of my line"[66] refers to their innumerable phone calls. "You steamed to me over the sea, / Fat and red, a placenta / Paralyzing the kicking lovers" alludes to her mother's visit to Plath and Ted Hughes's home in England the summer before their separation. When forging a self of power, you need to be hard. Her mother's sympathy for her situation must have been regarded by Plath as a temptation to weakness. In a letter to her mother written one week before the poem, Plath says that she won't be coming to America for a long time because "the horror" of what her mother saw and what she saw her mother see the previous summer would create a strain between them.[67] It is imperative to bury your heart in creating a self of power. A mother's sympathy— like the sympathy of Enki's creatures for Ereshkigal—can penetrate your defenses and leave your heart exposed. Plath had no intention of being vulnerable again. "Who do you think you are a Communion wafer? . . . / I shall take no bite of your body, / Bottle in which I live." But the poem no more frees Plath from her mother than "Daddy" freed her from her father and her husband. Curses always boomerang. The heart's release is the only thing that lets us walk away from people we have needed desperately. And Plath admitted, in the letter to her mother written the week before "Medusa," that it was only in heaven that she expected to find "what was [her] heart."

What could be more dangerous than losing touch with your heart? "Divorce is like an amputation," says the protagonist of Margaret Atwood's *Surfacing*. "You survive, but there's less of you."[68] The story of *Surfacing* is of a woman recovering her capacity to feel after a traumatizing separation from her lover. A woman who cannot feel cannot fall in love. And if you are not in love—with someone or something—life begins to seem like a great effort. Some women turn to the idea of God, at this point, hoping to find peace by contemplating the eternal. Not Plath.

> O God, I am not like you
> In your vacuous black,
> Stars struck all over, bright stupid confetti.
> Eternity bores me,
> I never wanted it.[69]

A woman who thrives on the feeling of power will not find peace appealing—at least not while there is still a way for her to feel powerful. "What I love is / The piston in motion—" Plath continues, "My soul dies before it. And the hooves of the horses, / Their merciless churn." Letting the hag-queen take over in your life makes you available to the power that is the opposite of the power of eros. Instead of propelling you into engagement with the things of life, it impels your withdrawal.

When your heart is broken—when the person to whom you have given your heart walks out on you—there is still your soul, with its wild desire—the hag's desire—that marriage could never satisfy. Alternating with the anger of the "October poems," there is a desire expressed that is sometimes wild and sometimes unbearably sweet. It is the desire to depart this world, to leave the body, to become pure spirit. It is as if Plath's attempt to forge a self of power in the face of death had its ultimate motivation in the realization that the alternative was to succumb to this desire. Here is the danger of losing touch with your heart: while the heart knows that death is the ultimate enemy, the unintegrated soul sees death as the ultimate ecstasy. Reading the poem, "Ariel," we like to picture Plath riding the horse to whom she gave that name. In its opening verses, it simply evokes the oneness of horse and rider. But there is a shift in the middle of the poem—"Something else / Hauls me through air—" and we know immediately where she is going. "The child's cry" is the last hook and then she is riding death:

> And I
> Am the arrow,
>
> The dew that flies
> Suicidal, at one with the drive
> Into the red
>
> Eye the cauldron of morning.[70]

A person does not have to be in a personal crisis to be susceptible to the power of death. Leo Tolstoy, at the age of fifty, happily married and happily employed, wrote of the experience of a great rupture with the life he knew:

> I felt that something had broken within me on which my life had always rested, and that I had nothing left to hold on to, and that morally, my life had stopped. An invincible force impelled me to get rid of my existence in one way or another. It cannot be said exactly that I *wished* to kill myself, for the force which drew me away from life was fuller, more powerful, more general than any mere desire. It was a force like my old aspiration to live, only it impelled me in the opposite direction. . . .[71]

Tolstoy used the term "call" to describe this experience. In "Lady Lazarus," Plath uses the same term, mockingly:

> Dying
> Is an art, like everything else.
> I do it exceptionally well.
>
> I do it so it feels like hell.
> I do it so it feels real.
> I guess you could say I've a call.[72]

The poem describes Plath's suicide attempts. She is bragging about her ability to submit to the power of death and come back to life. It is a feat, she implies, to ride death so far before pulling back. This is exactly what Inanna does, of course, on her underworld journey. In this respect, we can think of Ninshubur, who sounds the alarm among the gods when the goddess has been gone for three days, as corresponding to that controlling spirit which allows one's flirtation with death to go only up to a point. Lady Lazarus assures us that she is always in control. Anyone poking around her ashes thinking she is dead is in for a surprise:

> Herr God, Herr Lucifer
> Beware
> Beware.

> Out of the ash
> I rise with my red hair
> And I eat men like air.

In "Lady Lazarus," the two themes that characterize the last months of Plath's life come together: the desire to forge a self of power with the hag's rage and the desire to ride the power of death into oblivion. The self-mocking tone of "Lady Lazarus" hints that the latter desire is winning. "Purdah," a poem completed the same day as "Lady Lazarus," is the last of the angry poems.[73] It portrays a woman plotting the murder of her husband. Subsequent poems emphasize the fascination with death, while the controlling spirit that enables Lady Lazarus to flaunt her suicide attempts seems to slacken. In "Death and Co." the speaker is motionless and speechless before two men who want something from her.[74] The one, like a bird of prey, looks upon her as "red meat"; the other "Masturbating a glitter / . . . wants to be loved." The end of the poem sounds the fatalistic note we do not want to hear:

> The frost makes a flower,
> The dew makes a star,
> The dead bell,
> The dead bell.
>
> Somebody's done for.

The poems written to her children in the last months convey the tenderness of a mother who foresees her child's cruel and ineluctable destiny. "Mary's Song" likens her ten-month-old son to Jesus, ending with the line, "O golden child the world will kill and eat."[75]

Once a person has begun to envision her absence from this life, the pull of death can become very strong. It is like anticipating your departure from a place where you have been unhappy. The other place, however unknown, gleams in your mind like heaven. When the self is the arena of this unhappiness—when you cannot bear to be what you are, a woman re-

jected, a woman alone—the pull of death makes going on in
life an agony. "How far is it?" the speaker asks in "Getting
There."[76] "There is mud on my feet, / Thick, red and slipping.
It is Adam's side / This earth I rise from, and I in agony." The
poem depicts a military transport train on its way to the battle-
field. The speaker just wants to die and can't understand why
she should have to go through the trouble of combat:

> It is so small
> The place I am getting to, why are there
>   these obstacles—
> The body of this woman
> Charred skirts and deathmask
>
> And now detonations—
> Thunder and guns.
> The fire's between us.

"Getting There" is reminiscent of some of Plath's earlier poems
which express the desire to join her dead father. She describes
carriages heading towards battle as "cradles" and she pictures
herself, after the fighting is over, being reunited with her father in death.

> And I, stepping from this skin
> Of old bandages, boredoms, old faces
>
> Step to you from the black car of Lethe,
> Pure as a baby.

"Getting There" associates the wheels of the boxcars
which are "fixed to their arcs like gods" with "the silver leash
of the will— / Inexorable. . . ." "And their pride," the poem
continues, "all the gods know is destinations." The will to
power hurtles you forward in life, Plath seems to be saying, but
to what purpose? There is a hint, here, of the alienation of
Plath from her self of power which appears unmistakably in
the final poems. In this, she is like Will Barrett, the main
character in Walker Percy's novel, *The Second Coming,* who,
at the age of fifty, realizes that the self he has forged over twenty

years of serious effort means nothing to him. Like Plath, he had forged a self in anger—anger at his father, anger at death—and now, looking back over his life, it seems that "The whole twenty years could just as easily have been a long night's dream."[77] Whatever energy you expend in crafting a self of power, it can be very easy to walk away from it. To be rooted in your life, you have to love what you are doing—you have to have given it your heart. In *The Second Coming*, Will Barrett has never given his heart to anything. Plath, we know, with the dissolution of her marriage, was suffering a broken heart. When the anger of the late poems is spent, her pain reappears: "It is a heart, / This holocaust I walk in."[78]

When the true self is a self of pain and the power of death seems irresistible, a person may finally turn, with interest, to the idea of God. Compared to those images that attach you tenuously to this life—your child's face, the dawn breaking—the idea of God is like a pillar to which you can fasten your soul. The soul that is occupied with that idea no longer feels the fascination of death. The heart is still broken, but it has ceased manufacturing images of oblivion. A poem written on February 1, 1963, ten days before she died, indicates that Plath had mystical experiences late in her life, and her husband, reportedly, confirms this.[79] It is probable that they occurred after she wrote "Years," the poem of November 16th in which she refers derisively to God. "O God, I am not like you / in your vacuous black, / Stars stuck all over, bright stupid confetti" has the tone of someone castigating a God she doesn't know. But the February 1st poem, "Mystic," is poignant in its evocation of the letdown that can follow religious ecstasy:

> Once one has seen God, what is the remedy?
> Once one has been seized up
>
> Without a part left over,
> Not a toe, not a finger, and used,
> Used utterly, in the sun's conflagrations, the stains
> That lengthen from ancient cathedrals
> What is the remedy?[80]

But the idea of God seems not to have penetrated Plath's soul. Her final poems convey the detachment of someone who has already let go of her life.

A mystical experience is an experience of the living God in which the soul encounters God directly and not through something else. Immediate contact with the reality of God frees you of false conceptions of God you may have. When Plath, in response to the news of her father's death, declared to her mother, "I'll never speak to God again," she seems to have had in mind the kind of indifferent God she portrays in "Years"—the "great Stasis," according to one verse, who seems to gaze unmoved by human affairs from his "vacuous black." But when you have been "seized up / Without a part left over" as Plath puts it in "Mystic," it is impossible to think of God as indifferent. There is a newly tender spot in your soul which is proof of the supernatural love you experienced. However touched Plath was by her mystical experience, she did not emerge from it, apparently, ready to say Yes to her life and her broken self. It is as though Ereshkigal, despite the moment of grace in which her heart is touched by the sympathy of Enki's creatures, were to remain in the underworld instead of coming back to the land of the living. Her mystical experiences gave Plath a new vision of things. "Meaning leaks from the molecules," she writes, "The chimneys of the city breathe,"[81] evoking the transparency of ordinary reality in light of a perception of transcendence. But the lyricism of the stanzas of "Mystic" is broken by the matter-of-fact pronouncement with which it concludes: "The heart has not stopped."

If mystical experience reconciles me with Being, it does not solve the problem of my being; if it gives me a taste of eternal life, it does not relieve me of the burden of my life. Even the Living God is powerless to effect my choice for my life.

"Give your heart to your life," a wise man said once, when I complained of having a great heart but no object worthy of devotion. I appreciated his words, but I couldn't act upon them. All I could do was persist in believing that my longing for a "true love" was not in vain and that someday, just as the fairy tales promised, he would appear. It is the image of a true love—of being with her true love—that tends to sustain a woman's self. Destroy that image and she is delivered a death-blow to her self-esteem. Like most women, Sylvia Plath was no feminist. Instead of telling herself how she ought to feel when her husband abandoned her for another woman, she chose to be true to her feelings. But unlike most women, she could not resurrect her faith in fairy tales—maybe because, as her early poetry attests, her identification with the fairytale mode had always been ironic. A little girl who loses her adored father will never wholly trust the dream of "true love." Plath's last poems indicate that she never found a substitute for that dream. "Is there no great love," she asks in "Mystic," "only tenderness?"[82] Life without a man, unmediated existence—unthinkable, she seems to be saying. (In "Lesbos," one of the nastiest poems in *Ariel,* she heaps scorn on the idea of her taking a female lover.[83]) Women who live by the myth of true love will die by that myth when they find themselves alone, unable to believe that they will ever have a lasting relationship.

In "Tale of a Tub," Plath proclaimed her horror of unmediated existence, "absolute fact." Letting the hag-queen become dominant in her psyche while her husband became a dark god was her way of preserving mediation when he abandoned her. She seems to have felt both doomed to "play the hag," as we put it, and to have experienced the hag as a means of deliverance from a life without myth. What is the cost to a woman who plays the hag despairingly? She gets to the point, Plath's last poems indicate, where the pull of death cannot be resisted. "Sheep in Fog," completed on January 28, 1963, reveals that Plath finally surrendered to the attraction of death.

> My bones hold a stillness, the far
> Fields melt my heart.
>
> They threaten to let me through to a heaven
> Starless and fatherless, a dark water.[84]

In this poem, there is no romanticizing of death as the means by which she and her father will be reunited. Such a gloss, which makes the desire to exit this life less shocking, has been discarded. The image of the train from "Getting There" appears in the final poems, but it is now explicitly an image of futility. "It's running is useless," we find out in "Totem." "It will be eaten nevertheless."[85] "Getting There" associates the train with "destinations," but "There is no terminus," Plath writes in "Totem," "only suitcases / Out of which the same self unfolds like a suit."

Maybe a woman begins to die the minute she resigns herself to playing the hag—the minute she despairs of ever finding a true love. If Sylvia Plath is typical—and it strikes me that she may simply be the extreme case—the modern woman tends to live in the split between the child and the hag, between the expectation of a true love who will take away her aloneness and rage and grief over the absence of a true love, over being alone. What is interesting is that at both standpoints, true love eludes us. For the child, it is in the future; for the hag, it is in the past. We remember that when Plath was married, for all she claimed that her love for Ted Hughes was her "song," it did not seem to fulfill her; it did not keep her from dreaming and longing for her dead father. It is ironic, then—but how true to experience—that life became unbearable for her when their marriage ended. Her husband, at least, had signified her true love; when he was gone, she had no choice but to play the hag for her true love was in the past and now, because of her history of abandonment, the past seemed irretrievable. Sylvia Plath's suicide can be seen as the overt expression of what many women feel—that once you have lost a true love or what promises to be a true love and have no hope of retrieving it—your life is over. Why couldn't she live for her poetry? we protest. But a woman's work—in itself—falls outside the myth of true love. In "Words," written on February 1, 1963, Plath reveals how little significance her poetry came to have for her:

Axes
After whose stroke the wood rings,
And the echoes!
Echoes traveling
Off from the center like horses.

Years later I
Encounter them on the road—

Words dry and riderless
The indefatigable hoof-taps.[86]

In another poem written the same day, we find, "The blood jet is poetry, / There is no stopping it."[87] At the end of her life, Plath was writing because it was effortless for her. It was also, apparently, irrelevant. The conclusion of "Words" is sheer fatalism: "From the bottom of the pool, fixed stars / Govern a life."

What keeps coming to mind as I read Plath's final poems is a dream of mine that I have already described in which a child is going through room after room of her house looking for her mother only to come upon a hag-figure who grabs her in a smothering embrace. In my dream, the child wrestles free of the hag and runs out into the dark hallway still crying, "Mother, mother." In Plath's story, the child never breaks free of the hag. The despair in the last poems is palpable. The poem that begins "Your clear eye is the one absolutely beautiful thing," which Plath wrote to her little son or daughter, goes on to lament that all that fills the child's gaze is a "troublous / Wringing of hands [a] dark / Ceiling without a star."[88] There is dignity in the final poems, but it is the dignity of someone who has given up the fight and is waiting, calmly, to leave the arena. In "Edge," one of the last two poems she wrote, she portrays what can only be her death as a finished piece of work:

The woman is perfected.
Her dead

Body wears the smile of accomplishment,
The illusion of a Greek necessity

Flows in the scrolls of her toga.
Her bare

Feet seem to be saying
We have come so far, it is over.[89]

After this tragic tableau, we are not surprised to see that "Edge" ends with a scene reminiscent of "The Moon and the Yew Tree," the poem in which Plath first declared her identification with the hag:

The moon has nothing to be sad about,
Staring from her hood of bone.

She is used to this sort of thing.
Her blacks crackle and drag.

The Child and the Mother: Joan Didion, Mary Gordon, Virginia Woolf

The dream of true love—how absurd it can seem when love is absent from your life—but how vital it can be, Plath's story suggests, to a woman's sense of self. We must look at the figure of the child, who carries that dream in a woman's psyche, with new respect. On reflection, it seems that the dream of true love symbolizes what Simone Weil calls "the Good" and hanging on to the dream amounts to believing in the triumph of good over evil. "Deep in the heart of every human being," Weil writes, "from earliest infancy until the tomb, there is something that goes on indomitably expecting, in the teeth of all experience of crimes committed, suffered, and witnessed, that good and not evil will be done to him." She goes on to assert that "it is this, above all, that is sacred in human beings."[1] The triumph of good over evil, of course, is the main theme of fairy tales: the princess always gets her prince. Contrary to what we initially assumed, the fairytale mode, as much as it represents a certain repression of instinct, corresponds to something of the highest value: our connection to the Good. The case of Sylvia Plath indicates that to lose this connection is disastrous.

It is one thing, however, to relate to the Good through the symbol of true love—to believe that you will get your prince—and another to relate to the Good as Simone Weil describes: to believe "in the teeth of all experience of crimes committed, suffered, and witnessed"—that good and not evil will be done to you. It is the difference between trusting your luck—as in "fortune favors the brave"—and trusting in the Living God. There is such a thing as growing up with a princess self-conception, having the sense of being marked out for a special destiny. It is not so much beauty or talent or wealth that makes a young girl feel this way, but the conviction that whatever she longs for with all her heart she will get. As she looks around her, it seems to such a person that a passionate existence is rare, that all the older people she knows have settled for something less than a great love. When Sylvia Plath asked, "Is there no great love, only tenderness?"[2] she was giving voice to the princess's conviction that only a passionate existence is worthy of her. Should such a person lose her prince— as Plath did—it will seem as though an abyss has opened up in her life, that she is like a lost child crying in the dark.

A woman at such a juncture is on the point of a great adventure, of making the journey from trusting her luck to trusting in the Living God. But it is a journey that requires going into the dark, and for that reason many women never make it. "There is a child in me that is always crying"[3] the actress Liv Ullman writes in her autobiography *Changing*. She portrays her life as in flux—ebbing and flowing between intimacy and aloneness, between her relationships and her work so that the mournful child seems to be the constant in all her life's phases. Ullman, at least, acknowledges the crying child. How many women bury her and go on with their lives, pretending that the loss of their true love and the passionate existence he promised is something less than a catastrophe? They are like Orual, in C. S. Lewis's *Till We Have Faces*, who tries to forget her great loss by boarding up the well with the swinging chains that sound like a child's wailing late at night and throwing herself into her role as queen of Glome. This kind of woman may achieve a great deal and make a significant contribution to the well-being of others—the way Orual provides for the security of her people by establishing favorable alliances with neighboring kingdoms—but the real task, the spiritual task of her life remains unfinished.

What is the spiritual task of a woman's life? The Demeter-Persephone myth portrays it as the effort of becoming whole, of healing the split between the child and the mother in a woman's psyche—between being carefree and having a care—through a journey that climaxes in a confrontation with the void. According to this, when a woman ignores her crying child, she is refusing the journey to her own essential self, the point at which all the different aspects of a woman—the child-woman, the mother, and the wise woman or crone—are in harmony. The "cry for wholeness" as we might call it is a key element in certain modern women's stories. As in the myth, there is a sunlit meadow experience, in which mother and child are together, followed by a rupture. The authors diverge on the questions of whether and how wholeness can be attained. Joan Didion's *Book of Common Prayer* ends with mother and daughter unreconciled. The mother dies calling her lost child's name. In Mary Gordon's *The Company of Women*, mother and daughter are reunited when the daughter becomes a mother. *To the Lighthouse,* by Virginia Woolf, portrays a meeting of the mother who has died with the daughter—really, the daughter-figure—who longs for her in the eternal dimension. Each author tells a story that any woman, driven by her crying child, could enact.

THE SEARCH FOR THE SUNLIT MEADOW

From Sylvia Plath's story, we know that the anguish of the crying child can lead to despair. When her husband left, she took the desperate step of allowing the hag, allowing the destructive force of her rage, to take over in her life. A woman identifies with the hag as a last resort—when she has abandoned hope of ever being cured of her anguish. Many women, however, learn the trick of denial. When they sense the void in the experience of loss, instead of confronting it, they instinctively look away, refusing to admit their pain and dread to consciousness. Such women live outside themselves, so to speak, for all their unfulfilled desire gets projected onto an image of perfection which distracts them from the task of becoming whole. They take the image of their lost love as an icon and turn their hearts into shrines to its memory. By shielding them from the void, the image sustains their child-like expectation that "everything will turn out all right." Instead of moving forward in her life, the woman in denial is concerned to repeat beautiful moments from her past in which it seems to her that she was perfectly happy. In terms of the myth, she is facing in the opposite direction from that of Demeter: back to the sunlit meadow.

The figure of Charlotte Douglas, in Joan Didion's *Book of Common Prayer*, is a woman in search of the sunlit meadow. When her daughter Marin goes underground with a revolutionary terrorist group, she sets out on a journey that ends in Boca Grande—a country on the equator—where she waits for her daughter until she—Charlotte—is killed in a political uprising. If Boca Grande corresponds to Demeter's temple (it is located, literally, where all temples are located, symbolically—at the center of the world), the story is structurally similar to the myth. But the lack of reconciliation between mother and daughter—and the mother's death—is a dramatically different outcome. After Charlotte dies, the narrator, who was Charlotte's friend and can be viewed as the Hecate figure of the story, visits Charlotte's daughter. Their exchange is hostile, but at one point the daughter bursts into tears. What Didion's account brings out is that the daughter's sense of abandonment is due to her mother's lifelong pattern of denial. And denial, it seems, had been the hallmark of Charlotte's search. Instead of facing the void that her daughter's disappearance revealed, Charlotte had run from it—first, by trying to recapture the ecstasy of first love with her ex-husband and then by allowing herself to be lulled by the illusion that she and her daughter were "inseparable"[4]—that Marin's departure had not been voluntary and that the two of them would be reunited as soon as Marin could get free. The image Charlotte carried with her as an amulet against the void was the memory of Marin as a little girl entranced by the lights of the Tivoli Gardens in Copenhagen.

From the narrator's point of view, Charlotte was guilty of the unexamined life. The narrator—Grace Strasser-Mendana, a retired anthropologist—calls herself a "student of delusion."[5] She was drawn to Charlotte as the most striking case of self-delusion she had ever encountered. The portrait she paints of herself is of a woman as brutally honest about the human condition as Charlotte was dishonest. "Unlike Charlotte," she says, "I do not dream my life."[6] What she means is that she acknowledges the void; now dying of pancreatic cancer, she has lived in the lucid awareness of death since she was orphaned at the age of ten. Her reconstruction of those periods in Charlotte's life characterized by what Charlotte called the "separateness" is clearly a window on her own past:

> Of course there had been the usual days and weeks and even months when Charlotte had been separated from everyone she knew by a grayness so dense that the brightness of even her own child in the house was galling, insupportable, a reproach to be avoided at breakfast and on the stairs. During such periods Charlotte endured the usual intimations of erratic cell multiplication, dust and dry wind, sexual dysesthesia, sloth, flatulence, root canal. During such periods Charlotte would rehearse cheerful dialogues she might need to have with Marin. For days at a time her answers to Marin's questions would therefore strike the child as weird and unsettling, cheerful but not quite responsive. "Do you think I'll get braces in fourth grade," Marin would ask. "You're going to love fourth grade," Charlotte would answer. During such periods, Charlotte suffered the usual dread when forced to visit Marin's school and hear the

doomed children celebrate all things bright and beautiful all creatures great and small.[7]

The problem was, the narrator concludes, that Charlotte had no idea that any of this was "usual." Her denial sprang from the fact that she regarded her "separateness" as her own personal affliction.

The narrator's solution to the problem of death, of the void, is to expect nothing from life, neither the best nor, as so often happens when our dreams of the best are shattered, the worst. "I will die. . . ," she says, "neither hopeful nor its opposite."[8] Unlike the figure of Hecate in the myth, who is a cave-dwelling goddess, Grace "craves"[9] the light on Boca Grande, the "opaque, equatorial light"[10] which is "flat," "harsh," and "dead white at noon."[11] She prides herself on her unromantic assessment of the things and people around her. Where Charlotte, in one of her euphemistic "letters from Boca Grande," describes the country as a " land of contrasts," Grace sees it as "relentlessly the same." [12] She, too, has "lost" a child—her son Gerardo has become a cynical politician— but unlike Charlotte, she carries no shining image of him in her mind. Grace seems to think that there are two kinds of people: those like herself who can live without illusions and those like Charlotte who cannot. She registers disapproval toward all the characters in the narrative who set store by wealth or status or power as if any of these things could cancel our fundamental bondage to death. Instead of looking away from death as Charlotte does, she keeps it "in [her] line of sight, . . . under surveillance, . . . on cleared ground and away from any brush where it might coil unnoticed."[13]

As much as it chronicles Charlotte's life, A Book of Common Prayer is really about the self-revelation of the narrator. From the beginning of the story, we are led to wonder why Grace is drawn to the figure of Charlotte. But as the narrative unfolds, even as the obvious differences between Charlotte and Grace become apparent, we start to suspect an underlying affinity between the two women. Grace likes the fact that Charlotte, for all the money her husband had, was egalitarian. She relishes the story of her killing a chicken with her bare hands. In scene after scene, we see her sitting on the sidelines, keeping an almost protective watch over Charlotte, feeling an almost visceral pain when Charlotte runs up against something hard, when an obdurate piece of reality will not conform to her pretty picture of it. At every point, Grace's observations seem to distance her from Charlotte; nevertheless, she comes to her defense on occasion with the kind of passion that always indicates that we identify, somehow, with the person under attack. The turning point for the narrator is when the unconscious connection between her and Charlotte comes to light. She learns from Charlotte's husband (the Zeus figure of the story) who has come to Boca Grande to try to convince Charlotte to leave the island, that her deceased husband had been involved in arms trafficking. This surprises Grace because she had believed her husband to be unlike the rest of his family, who are all Machiavellian in their pursuit of power. In that moment she realizes that she, just as much as Charlotte, had been clinging to an illusion. The book ends soon after, with a pall of smoke obscuring the light in Boca Grande as the narrator is forced to rethink her assessment of Charlotte. "I am less and less certain," she says, "that this story has been one of delusion. Unless the delusion was mine."[14]

Didion's point in A Book of Common Prayer seems to be that we all need to believe in a sunlit meadow. We need to think that some aspect of our lives has been pure—set apart, like a gleaming jewel, from the everyday rubble. Charlotte's death, Grace comes to realize, was not due to her failure to read the signs that a military takeover of the island was imminent, but was the result, rather, of a deliberate choice to put herself in the line of fire. Having received the news that Marin was free but had refused to see her, Charlotte chose death over a life without the beautiful illusion of herself and Marin as inseparable. (At the moment of death, Grace learns,

Charlotte cried out "not for God but for Marin."[15]) The question arises, does *A Book of Common Prayer* represent any progress beyond Sylvia Plath's standpoint? If Charlotte dies despairing and Grace comes to the realization that she, too, has been unable to live without illusion, aren't we back at the juncture where the shattering of one's dream makes life meaningless? The woman who believes in the sunlit meadow differs from the princess awaiting her prince mainly in her orientation. Concerned to repeat, if only in her mind, something that has already happened, she is focused on the past, whereas the princess locates the perfect moment in the future: however often she has been disappointed, the princess is always waiting for her life to begin. (The disappointments, she tells herself, were false starts.) Both are vulnerable to the turn of events that can extinguish their hope: the one to the discovery that her image of the past is an illusion, the other to rejection by the person she settles on as her prince.

Sometimes it happens that a story is wiser than any of its characters. While it is true that neither Charlotte nor Grace experiences illumination in the course of the novel, the reader reflecting on the way the book ends can be illumined. When mother and daughter are in the underworld, the story seems to be saying, when the heart of a woman, her feelings and sensuality, have been submerged by despair, there is still her power of mind—what the narrator, the Hecate figure represents. By reflecting on the change that occurs in the narrator as she tells Charlotte's story—and taking it one step further—we can find in the ending of *A Book of Common Prayer* a glimmer of hope. The narrator lives her life in the awareness of death and that awareness is characterized by dread. Death for her is a snake coiled up in the brush, an enemy that can strike at any moment. It is because of her fear of death that she "craves the light." When someone lives in dread, she sees things with what Sylvia Plath called her "ice eye."[16] The "ice eye" scrutinizes people with a dissecting gaze that negates all sense of connection, of fellow-feeling. Throughout the book, Grace calls herself *de afuera*—an outsider. She says that she has been *de afuera* all her life—ever since her parents died and she lived by herself in the Brown Palace Hotel in Denver. Being *de afuera*, she seems to think, gives her an objectivity regarding events and people in Boca Grande that everyone around her lacks. Her realization, at the end of the book, that she has not understood Charlotte Douglas is momentous in that it seems to represent not just a questioning of a particular judgment she has made about a person, but real doubt as to whether what she means by objectivity has any relation to the truth. One of the last things the narrator tells us about Charlotte is that she was detained at the *Escuela de los Ninos Perdidos*—the school for lost children—before she was shot to death. The pall of smoke that surrounds the narrator in the final scene seems to symbolize her recognition that she, too, is lost.

Admitting you are lost, that you don't know the truth—this can dispel the influence of the "ice eye." We have been prepared for such an admission by Grace since the beginning of the book. Her opening statement announces, "I will be her witness,"[17] but clues us in to the intractability of the problem she poses: discerning the meaning of a person's life. She is an anthropologist, she tells us, who "lost faith in her own method, who stopped believing that observable activity defined anthropos."[18] After producing some "well-regarded" studies on the rearing of female children in the Mato Grosso, she "still did not know why any one of these children did or did not do anything at all." Moreover, she "did not know why [she] did or did not do anything at all."[19] Now, at the age of sixty and dying, she has taken Charlotte as one last study, as much to learn about herself, we come to realize, as to learn about Charlotte. Her closing statement, "I have not been the witness I wanted to be"[20] is poignant, for the subtext is clearly, "I am not the person I thought I was." The narrator's name—Grace—invites us to take this admission of failure in a hopeful direction. To know that you don't know, as Socrates pointed out, is wisdom. The discovery that you are lost, the Christian writer Walker Percy maintains, is the beginning of your path. The admission of ignorance first of all frees us from the rigidity of a life based on assumptions about the truth and secondly, disposes us to wonder. Wonder is what dread becomes when we reflect on our experience of death. Reflected upon, death is not the enemy we assume from the nightmarish shapes it takes in our imaginations, but rather, the unknown.

When wonder at the unknown replaces our dread of death, the mind sees possibilities where it used to see gaps and possibility is like air to the spirit. Spirit may first emerge in a woman, that is, a woman may first become conscious of herself as spirit—as having a life beyond that of her emotions and her body—through the experience of dread. If, like the narrator, we face in the direction of death, of the void, and refuse to turn away from that reality, there comes a moment when the thrall of our projections is broken and we get a glimpse of mystery. Spirit in us is stifled by projections, by lying. That any earthly thing can protect us from the power of death, that any earthly thing is perfect—free of the flaws endemic to finite existence—is a lie. If we face the reality of death unflinchingly, sooner or later, we stop lying. Facing death indicates a desire to live in the truth and it is this desire, Simone Weil says, that is always efficacious. What saves the narrator—and I persist in thinking that if the book continued, we would find Grace emerging from the pall of smoke and gazing contemplatively toward the horizon—is her desire for truth. If our desire for truth means that our dread of death initially causes us to see the world with our "ice eye," it also means that eventually we will come to wonder at the world, at the mystery of death.

THE LIGHT OF COMMON DAY

A woman rejoining the human circle, after the experience of loss has isolated her, feels like a ghost—her spirit haunting her body—until her heart can make a connection to another body which restores her to her own. Instead of choosing the dispassionate life of spirit, which is a real option for anyone quickened by wonder, she wants to choose what she regards as a more human life. Her heart is broken; images of the life of spirit lack the power to knit it together, but the image of home and family, the image of a child, make it lunge like a hungry dog. Who can blame a woman for trying to satisfy this hunger? It makes her feel alive again—as the quickening of her spirit does not—and promises access to the simple human warmth one never takes for granted after a sojourn in the underworld. Mary Gordon's novel, *The Company of Women*, explores the question of what kind of life is possible for a woman in the aftermath of disaster. The main character, Felicitas, is a Persephone figure. She rebels against her Catholic mother and her mother's world by having an affair with her political science professor, with whom she is passionately in love. Robert loses interest in her just about the time that she discovers she is pregnant. Unable to go through with an abortion, she is forced to return home. For two years, she suffers a deep depression, refusing to touch or hold her baby. Finally, she responds to the "gravitational pull"[21] of the child and begins a new life centered on her love for her daughter.

What Mary Gordon refers to as the "gravitational pull," we have referred to elsewhere as the life-force. In the aftermath of a tragic love affair—where you have given your heart, let us say, like Felicitas, when it was unwanted—if the life-force surges up again, there is the chance to build a new life. But this re-entry into relationship is as different from the passionate self-surrender of first love as day from night. Indeed, like Charles, when he was leaving Brideshead at the end of his relationship with Sebastian, a woman at this juncture may feel that she has "come to the surface, into the light of common day."[22] Instead of seeming awesome and irresistible, the life-force apart from the whole heart's passion seems simply vital—necessary to human existence but not its glory. Nevertheless, like the narrator of *A Book of Common Prayer* "craving" the light in Boca Grande, a woman can find that she craves the person with whom she has this vital connection. Mothers say to their children, "I could eat you up I love you so much." And this expresses it well, for a mother's need for her child can be one of those needs of the soul which Simone Weil describes that are exactly analogous to our need for food.[23] It is no wonder that a woman returning from the underworld will sometimes give birth to child after child. Her soul is famished and could suffer harm were she deprived of them.

Gordon's novel underlines the importance of being in touch with our needs. Its main male character is a priest—Father Cyprian—who chose the religious life out of a desire to transcend his fleshly nature. He was a farmer's son who wanted to trade his face of "flesh, soil, earth, the animal he was" for one that was "no face, but a clear transparency." He wanted to "give over the flesh he lived in, the strong muscles of his back, so that his soul could show through the sharp, visible bones of his breast."[24] But Cyprian's career turned out differently from what he had envisioned. At first, he was a popular preacher, drawing crowds by his zeal for the spiritual life. But when his superiors relaxed the requirements for living out his order's vows, he became alienated from his brother priests. He even knocked one unconscious when the younger man made a joke at his expense. Consigned to the upkeep of the plumbing in the monastery, he decided to leave. After four years in Arizona with the Indian missions, he asked to be re-assigned to his home diocese. When the book opens, Cyprian is living on his family's homestead saying Mass every day for one of the members of a group of women for whom he has been spiritual director ever since the days when his preaching was in demand. As much as he enjoys the company of these women, he never changes his view of himself as a failure. In his soliloquy at the end of the book, he laments that he has never been able to "disentangle [himself] from the passions, the affections." He has never been able to "love with a burning heart that demands only itself and never asks for gratitude or kindness." Instead, he has "hungered" for kindness, for gratitude.[25]

Though Gordon leaves the old priest in conflict over his situation, it is clear she believes that his life at the center of the circle of women—Felicitas's mother and her friends and Felicitas, too, after her loss and recovery—is blessed. She portrays Cyprian's priestly ideal as inhuman and his aspiring to it as a kind of hubris from which he is saved by his work on the land and his affection for the women. In the soliloquy that is a review of his life prompted by a heart attack that leaves him near death, Cyprian sees that "it was grandeur" he had wanted in joining the priesthood.[26] He had not wanted to be "the son of [his] father, the brother of [his] brothers, bumbling and heavy and uncouth." He had wanted to be "part of that glorious company, the line of the apostles."[27] But "his obligation in charity," he decides, had been to remain on the farm[28] and throughout his career, he realizes, he had consistently failed at charity. When penitents came to him, he had found himself loving them "not in God but for themselves . . . for the pleasure of words given and taken, personal gifts."[29] His love for his brother priests could not embrace their imperfections. But worst of all, he seems to think, had been the "terrible possessiveness" of his love for Felicitas, whom he had loved and continues to love as his own child. As Gordon sees it, it is the idea of an "impersonal, objective love" that is terrible, that has estranged Cyprian from himself and the people who love him. For years, Cyprian admits, he had regarded the friendship of the women as "second best," as a "pitiful travesty of the durable shining friendship [he] sought from another man."[30] But even now that he values their love, he can't forgive himself for needing it.

Real love, Gordon seems to be saying, has its roots in the flesh, in the things that make the other person attractive to us. There is a Yeats poem that ends "But only God my dear/ Could love you for your self alone/And not your yellow hair."[31] Gordon would not only agree, she would say that we damage ourselves by trying to love "purely"—by failing to take our needs and desires into account. Cyprian's attachment to the ideal makes him prone to self-hatred and the women feel his bitterness. Felicitas, though she is like Father Cyprian in some ways, having been a kind of spiritual prodigy of his as a child, is more comfortable in her love of her mother and the circle of friends to which the two of them belong. A woman who has suffered a serious depression knows what it is to have her heart closed shut against life. Felicitas says she understands mothers "who starve their children, who beat them . . . who leave babies in shopping bags in the post office."[32] She and her child were saved by the kindness of the women who surrounded them at that time. If maternal instinct in the women fueled their kindness, it seems no less a "miracle" to Felicitas. Human blessedness, human happiness consists, for Mary Gordon, in the strength of our human ties. Muriel, the most spiritual of the women around Father Cyprian, is the least happy because no one really desires her companionship. She waits, she admits, "for the singular gaze, the gaze of permanent choosing . . ." and she, too, is bitter—from knowing that she will die "the first beloved of no living soul."[33]

The need to be the center of another person's life. If this is what we most desire, then motherhood is the ideal state for human beings. A beloved creature—utterly dependent on my care—how the circle of our relationship seems to fill the void at the center of myself. Felicitas recovers from her tragic love affair by substituting her passion for her child for her unrequited passion for Robert. The man she decides to marry—Leo Byrne who works in a hardware store—does not arouse passion in her, but promises to be a good father. The passion Felicitas arouses in him gives him the status of another needy creature who is dependent on her. In relations between men and women, Gordon seems to think, it is women who are the stronger. Their more instinctual nature equips them for being guardians of life. When Cyprian wakes up in the middle of the night from a dream about the monastery, he sets off in the dark wanting to flee "the muffling, consoling flesh" of the women around him.[34] But he gets only as far as an all-night diner, where a waitress who offers him a cup of coffee and calls him "dear" makes him feel like Tobias encountering the angel. In his soliloquy, he expresses concern that his dying will leave his women friends "alone in spirit, un-shepherded,"[35] but this is almost ironic, for the soliloquy is mainly a confession that it is he who is dependent on them. "I am doomed like the rest of my kind," is how he puts it, "to the terrible, ringed accident of human love. I am pulled down by the irresistible gravity of affection and regard."[36]

The superiority of women, Gordon would say, is that they tend to say yes to the life-force instead of resisting it like Cyprian. Felicitas is different from the other women mainly in that she is doing self-consciously and deliberately what they have always done without reflecting upon it. As Catholic women and disciples of Father Cyprian, they have tried very hard to "banish instinct from their lives"[37] but in a crisis, they rely on it. Felicitas's Catholicism seems to be dead after her experience of the underworld. She identifies in herself a "hard, leaden center upon which the word of God would not catch fire, but freeze."[38] Yet in her soliloquy, we find out that her passionate concern for her daughter and their circle of friends is colored by her passionate rejection of the Catholic God. She sees the world as full of "danger"[39] with human life and love threatened at every point. Like Cyprian, she can conceive of God only as "pure light"[40] detached from the contingencies of human existence, but unlike Cyprian, she cannot love a God who is detached. "I will not let Him into my heart," she says. "My daughter is there, my mother, Leo, Cyprian, the women whom I love. I will not open my heart to God . . . I will not submit myself."[41] She admits that she "hungers" for a "perception of the sacred," for the "clear, the unencumbered."[42] But this seems to be a desire of the mind she is willing to forego in the face of the urgency of her heart's imperative.

The recovered heart wants life, according to Mary
Gordon, and a God we associate simply with the mind's illumination seems opposed to life. The woman whose spirit has
been quickened by wonder can conceive of God only as light.
Wonder is precisely an intimation of illumination, the sense
that one's desire to know is not in vain, that it will never out-
strip the truths to be discovered, the mysteries to be revealed.
It must have been people imbued with wonder who first wor-
shipped the "God of the shining sky" that Marija Gimbutas
has identified as the deity of the peoples who invaded the
centers of goddess-worshipping civilization and destroyed
them.[43] There is an inevitable conflict between the God of
the shining sky and the Goddess—it is the conflict we feel
between the pull of the life of spirit which draws us beyond
the human circle and the pull of the life-force which binds us
to it. If Felicitas feels this conflict, she is resolute in her
choice of the latter. Where Cyprian suffers his involvement
in the "flesh," his dependence on particular friendships,
human ties, Felicitas makes her choices and defends them on
the basis of her human ties. About her decision to marry Leo
she admits that she "find[s] it difficult to justify [her] reverence for a man of so little mind," but she "wants to be more
human,"[44] she wants her daughter to have a father. A woman
who has experienced the shattering of her dream and sur-
vived that loss knows that whatever God we believe in we
are all vulnerable to death. If she wonders at the meaning of
death, she feels instinctively that the worthiest task for human
beings is to shield each other from death as much as possible.
A fatherless child is "unsheltered," Felicitas believes. She will
marry Leo for "shelter."[45]

What is being celebrated in the final scene of the book
where Felicitas and her mother are standing under an apple
tree, laughing as Felicitas's little girl runs toward them is the
renewing power of the life-force. The little girl—Linda—has
the last word: "I run out. I can feel my heart. I am running

toward them. . . . My mother picks me up and holds me in her arms. . . . My grandmother is laughing. My mother lifts me up into the leaves. We are not dying."[46] We should exult in every upsurge of the life-force, Gordon indicates. We should rejoice—just like our goddess-worshipping ancestors—in the predictable but ever-marvelous reappearance of the life-force after a period of death. Felicitas loves Linda not only for the child herself but because her own life has been renewed through that of her child. Cyprian, facing death, realizes that it had been the birth of Linda that had "brought [him] back to life" that had restored his faith in God's "loving providence." The child had been a sign that Felicitas "would come back" to them and they would "prosper."[47] Gordon passes lightly over the turning point of the story—the moment when Felicitas opens her heart to her child and to life after being shut up in despair for months. "I cannot even recall," Felicitas says, "what happened to me, why my own life changed. Someone came for a visit, said the right thing, brought the right gifts, and somehow I was no longer desperate."[48] The life-force surges up in us when it does, Gordon implies. We should be simple enough to enjoy the new life that presents itself.

As a retelling of the Demeter-Persephone myth, *The Company of Women* is not about wholeness, but rather, initiation: it shows how an experience of the underworld can make us strong. The focus is not on a mother losing and recovering her child, but on the child losing her innocence—her belief that her dreams will be fulfilled—and becoming a mother. Felicitas's mother doesn't change in the course of the novel; she and the other women simply wait for Felicitas to take her place among them. The spiritual task for women, according to Gordon, is to make the transition from daughter to mother—from being carefree to having a care, as we have put it. Making that transition involves acquiring a knowledge of death, for only with the awareness of death do we truly value the life-force. The mother or mature woman's responsibility, Gordon would say, is to cooperate with the life-force—to let it carry us into relationships and projects when it waxes and to wait, confident of its resurgence, when it wanes. Felicitas's mother experienced death when her husband—Felicitas's father—died in the second year of their marriage. Her ability to make plans and to change them, to uproot herself from her home and her job when her daughter's situation demands it, and above all, her "gift" of "not wanting what she [doesn't] have"[49] seem to have been reinforced by the experience of death. The child's yes to life is untempered: when the child realizes that her dream will not be fulfilled, she can turn in an instant from saying yes to saying no to life. But the mother's yes—forged in the crucible of disillusionment, according to Gordon—has something of steel in it. When Felicitas recovers from her loss, she is not a child anymore. The force of her caring is as ineluctable as her mother's.

Caring—caring tenaciously—about another human being, this is the antidote to despair that Gordon proposes. When Cyprian says to Felicitas from his hospital bed, "It hasn't been much of a life for you," she is "insulted." "I thought I had made a good life," she tells us in her soliloquy, "I was happier than I had ever been."[50] As much as her little girl can be understood to symbolize the new life that Felicitas embraces, the old priest seems to represent the life of spirit that she rejects. Hence their misunderstanding. What Felicitas resents is Cyprian's failure to recognize that there is spirit in the life she has chosen. There is spirit in caring—in taking another person into the circle of yourself. If it is an upsurge of the life-force that tricks you into opening yourself, making room for the other in your heart, it is an act of will that sustains the relationship, that knots the self around this person and not that one. "Marriage: it is a choice," Felicitas reflects "not an act of nature visited upon me."[51] Cyprian is anguished because his spirit can't soar beyond the "particular loves" that he needs; he feels that he has failed not only himself but God in this.

Felicitas would insist that relating responsibly to our "particular loves" is how we express the claim of God upon us. She affirms Margaret Fuller's statement, "I accept the universe," understanding it to be about "volition . . . about the central human struggle to place oneself in relation to the absolute."[52]

As a Persephone figure, Felicitas's loss and recovery do not go as deep as Demeter's. The transition from daughter to mother involves acquiring the will to live, the power of saying yes to the life-force even though we know, from painful experience, that life is "dangerous." Demeter's journey presupposes this power. There is no question of Demeter's will to live: from the moment she loses her daughter, she is given over to the search for her. But the search, as we interpreted it, culminates not simply in new life, but in a deeper life—a life in which all the different aspects of herself are in harmony. The turning point of her journey is a confrontation with the void, with death, which is simultaneously a confrontation with Zeus, which brings her to the point of unity in herself. As we have seen, the mature woman Felicitas becomes resists an encounter with God. The acts of will by which she "places [herself] in relation to the absolute" are actually choices that seem reasonable to her. "I will not look to God for comfort, or for succor or for sweetness," she says. "God will have to meet me on the high ground of reason."[53] Felicitas is content, apparently, with a self-constructed life, a life that she shapes so as to preserve and strengthen the relationships that mean everything to her. In the summing up at the end of her soliloquy, there is no mention of the kind of distress that drives Demeter to her showdown with Zeus. It is a sober statement which indicates that Felicitas accepts the confinement of the life against which she once rebelled:

> And I go on, the daughter of my mother, the mother of my daughter, caretaker of the property, soon to be a man's wife. My life is isolated, difficult, and formal. It is, perhaps, not the life I would have chosen, but it is a serious life. I do less harm than good.[54]

GIVING BIRTH TO YOUR DIVINE CHILD

A woman reflecting on the last words of Felicitas's soliloquy—recognizing herself, perhaps, in the subdued statement of the once exuberant girl—might begin to raise some troubling questions. What do women lose, she might ask, in refusing an encounter with the God of the shining sky? What price do we pay for devoting ourselves exclusively to the life-force and the relationships it engenders? The mature Felicitas is certainly passionate: she cares deeply for her child and their little community. And undeniably, as she says, she does more good than harm: a passionate mother imbues her children with the sense that life matters, that all the effort it takes to survive is worth it. Growing up with a parent with a strong will to live, a person feels that the unforgivable sin is to fail to do everything in her power to keep herself and her loved ones safe. In retrospect, it seems that it was the inexorable will to live of Felicitas's mother that was a crucial factor in her daughter's coming back from the underworld. Hers was not the sympathetic caring of a grandfather Enki—far from it. She and her daughter never discussed Felicitas's relationship with Robert. But the mother was relentless in her caring. Day in and day out for two years, Felicitas could see her feeding and rocking and bathing the baby. As miserable as she was, Felicitas's no to life could not prevail over her mother's yes. But once one has turned to life, once the will to live is as strong in one as a healthy animal, it is possible to feel that something is missing.

If Felicitas expresses no ambivalence about the life she has chosen, the protagonist of Gordon's next book, *Men and Angels*, who is like Felicitas but at thirty-eight, ten years older, is filled with self-doubt. *Men and Angels* can also be viewed as a variation on the Demeter-Persephone story. The three main characters—Laura, a young woman; Anne, a mature woman; and Jane, an old woman—correspond to the maid, mother, crone triumvirate of the myth. Central to the story is Anne's relationship with Laura. Having taken on an intellectual project while her husband is abroad, Anne hires Laura as a live-in governess for her two children. Despite her job in an art gallery and her credentials as an art historian, Anne defines herself through her role as mother. She is perplexed, consequently, when she finds herself unable to love Laura—an odd, needy person whose lack of human ties is painfully evident. Laura, for her part, falls in love with Anne. She imagines Anne leaving her husband so that the two of them can live together in their own little house. The novel comes to a tragic climax when Anne, in a fit of rage, dismisses Laura. The girl commits suicide and Anne has to live with the memory of Laura's blood in her house.

What does it mean, in the modern woman's story, when the mother rejects the wounded child? *Men and Angels* makes me think of a dream I had in which the opposite occurs. I was in the upstairs of my house, watching in dismay as it was being invaded by a group of "happy Christians" who were going to have a party. I fled to the basement where I found a deformed child lying in a coal bin, crying. As I stood over the child, I could feel her pain. When some of the group from upstairs found me in the basement and urged me to join their party, I refused. I knew I had to stay with the crying child. If the child is the dream-bearer in our psyches, a neglected, deformed child would signify the inability to dream—to transcend one's present situation in the hope of a shining future. A woman at mid-life, who may have prided herself on being past dreaming, on having exchanged her youthful idealism for achievable objectives and goals, is liable to wake up one morning with the feeling that she is dying inside. Her life has become what the theologian John Dunne calls a "deadly clear path."[55] She still loves the people on whom she has lavished her care, but caring for them is burdensome now and not energizing. Her heart is heavy as she faces the prospect of each new day. The question for a woman at this point is whether she will admit her inner pain and need for healing or deny that there is anything really wrong with her.

What is wrong with a woman who has lost her capacity to dream? Isn't real life, a responsible life, about renouncing one's impossible dreams and trying to accomplish some limited good? Isn't a flesh and blood husband to whom she is committed better than the prince who got away? Over and over a woman may tell herself these things, fearing that to acknowledge her unhappiness would be to undermine the structure of relationships she has worked so hard to build. In *Men and Angels*, Anne dismisses Laura because she threatens the safety of her household. She lets Anne's children play on untested ice. Normally mild-mannered, Anne becomes violently angry—actually hateful—toward Laura in this scene. But her outburst, though prompted by Laura's negligence, has been inevitable since their first meeting. Anne's initial uneasiness around Laura, she realizes later, should have been taken as a warning against letting Laura into her house. A woman's fear of contact with her wounded child, it seems, is basically the fear that her "house" is insubstantial: that the life she has created, the self she has forged, cannot withstand the expression of her deepest feelings. Anne is still afraid after Laura has died. In one of the last scenes of the book she finds Jane—the Hecate figure—sitting in the darkened living room of Anne's house contemplating the tragedy. Anne loves Jane but she can't endure her presence at this moment and runs upstairs to her bedroom and the protective embrace of her husband.

How to heal the wounded inner child! How to recover the sense of an open future when commitments seem to bind you to a "deadly clear path." The woman who fails to face this problem honestly runs the risk of becoming like Anne: turning to her relationships for refuge instead of a heart-to-heart exchange. The last scene of *Men and Angels* reminds me of a Rilke story in which a woman answers a knock on her door one morning to find the figure of Death on her doorstep. He has something to give her—a pouch of shiny black seeds—but she pulls away and slams the door shut. She says nothing to her husband about the visitor and tries to put him out of her mind. But little by little, her life changes. Friends begin to stay away from their cottage, the windows are closed to bird-song and fresh air, and she and her husband start avoiding each other's gaze. At night they sometimes wake up terrified—clinging to each other but saying not a word—at the sound of a loud knocking coming through the bedroom wall. There comes a time when a woman will lose all she has if she doesn't open herself to the reality of death. The crying child that she thought she had left behind when her princess self-conception gave way to the mother's resolve will alienate her from her life until she embraces her.

Revisiting your encounter with death! Going back to the break in your life between a sunlit childhood and an existence filled with care. What does that mean but letting yourself feel once again the loss that made you aware of the aloneness of human beings, of how we are fundamentally separate from each other so that all our dreams of the "beautiful fusion" of self and world that Sylvia Plath mentions[56] are futile. Death makes us solitary individuals. To revisit death is to feel once again the pain of that emergence—its mixture of dread and loneliness. Virginia Woolf's most celebrated novel, *To the Lighthouse*, which she began in 1925 at the age of forty-three, can be viewed as a revisiting of her most profound experience of loss—the death of her mother when she was thirteen. "Her death," she wrote, "was the greatest disaster that could happen."[57] It was followed by Woolf's first bout with mental illness. *To the Lighthouse* is a Demeter-Persephone story in the form of a child seeking her lost mother. Lily Briscoe, a young, spinsterly, aspiring artist—who is clearly modeled on Woolf herself—is the child figure. The object of her love is Mrs. Ramsay—the half goddess, half Victorian saint of a mother who, according to Woolf's sister, was the very likeness of their own mother. Part One of the book, "The Window," describes a sunlit meadow experience: Lily is with Mrs. Ramsay at the Ramsay's summer house in the Hebrides. Part Two, "Time Passes," marks the break in Lily's life between the wonder of that time and the starkly ordinary quality of her life since. In Part Three, "The Lighthouse," Lily makes the journey to the point in herself where she and Mrs. Ramsay, now dead, meet.

The novels Woolf wrote before *To the Lighthouse*, with their themes of rupture and aloneness, can be thought of as preliminary statements of the problem she addresses in her masterpiece. In *The Voyage Out*, completed shortly after Woolf was married, the young heroine dies shortly after she becomes engaged. *Night and Day*'s heroine, Katharine Hilbery, is re-solved on marriage at the end of the book, but only after her mother convinces her not to be dissuaded by the huge gaps in her feelings for the man who wants to marry her. *Mrs. Dalloway* presents the isolation of the insane person, Septimus Warren Smith, as the complement of the society matron, Mrs. Dalloway, and her effortless connection with people. The specter of nothingness raised in these books indicates that marriage had not filled the void for Woolf that the death of her mother had opened up. The novels hint at her fundamen-tal insecurity. Trying to explain to her mother why she feels she can't marry Ralph Denham, Katharine says:

> It seems as if something came to an end suddenly—gave out—faded—an illusion—as if when we think we're in love we make it up—we imagine what doesn't exist. That's why it's impossible that we should ever marry. Always finding the other an illusion, and going off and forgetting about them, never to be certain that you cared, or that he wasn't caring for someone not you at all, the horror of changing from one state to another.[58]

The feeling of lacking a substantial self—the sense that the face she shows to the world is not her real face—this is the cause of a woman's insecurity when she has nothing to put be-tween herself and the void. In *Night and Day*, Katherine and her mother "look . . . together into the abyss"[59] at the end of their conversation following Mrs. Hilbery's admission that she, too, has feelings of unreality. The women return, however, to the men who love them—the childlike Mrs. Hilbery focused firmly once more on the "ancient fairy tale"[60] of love, as Woolf calls it, that has sustained her in her marriage and Katharine ready to share a life with Ralph. We know that Katharine will not live by a fairy tale: her loneliness is part of her relationship with Ralph; her realization that he understands her loneliness seems to be the basis of her love for him. Instead of focusing on each other or their dreams of each other, the lovers look together toward the future, which appears to them "vast, mysterious, infinitely stored with undeveloped shapes which each would unwrap for the other to behold."[61]

Katharine and Ralph are not so much lovers, in the traditional sense, as fellow-voyagers into the unknown. Virginia and Leonard Woolf appear to have had the kind of partnership marriage that Katharine and Ralph envision. It is well known that after a disastrous honeymoon, they seem to have given up on sex, but they were widely reputed as one of the happiest couples in Bloomsbury. They spent most of their time together working on the Hogarth Press which they operated from their house and reading and critiquing each other's manuscripts. The letter Woolf left for Leonard the day she committed suicide concludes, "I don't think two people could have been happier than we have been."[62] A partnership marriage leaves you open to the void the way a romantic marriage does not. When you are focused on the other with desire and longing, nothing seems more powerful than your love. Your existence is constantly reaffirmed by the force of your passion. But when your marriage consists in looking together with the other instead of looking at the other, so that you have a clear view of the horizon, the winds of self-doubt can assume hurricane proportions.

In adulthood, Woolf's breakdowns tended to coincide with the completion of her novels. She was bed-ridden and delusional for months—even attempting suicide—after finishing *Night and Day*. What tormented her, according to her husband, was the thought that critics might reject her books.

Lacking children, she would then be without any external validation of her self-worth. A woman at this juncture instinctively withdraws. To act is impossible. If she has an unfinished encounter with death, all her energy is spent denying death access to the sanctuary of her heart.

Death is the perennially unfinished business for someone who has sustained a loss without grieving it through. If the old wise woman has come to your aid in surviving the loss—if your mind sees death as an endlessly fascinating riddle—the mother's heart in you can be shut tight against it. The figure of Woolf the writer—putting books rather than children between herself and the void—is a Demeter trying desperately to make Demophoon immortal. But Woolf on her sickbed is a Persephone in the underworld—feeling the power of death as close as a lover. Woolf's alternation between Demeter's desperation and Persephone's despair was extreme: few women are as narrowly focused as Woolf was in writing her novels (she told a friend that her writing was all she ever thought about), and few become as helpless as she did when she lost the focus of her work. But many of us live between desperation and despair: we pursue our life-projects with grim resolve and feel utterly worthless when we're not working. The most accomplished woman can be reduced to the state of a little lost child and then she realizes that for all her accomplishments, she has not budged an inch from that fairytale landscape where her father or lover or some other lost loved one is a numinous figure calling from beyond the boundary of death. Among the voices Woolf heard during her periods of insanity was that of her mother. For Woolf to emerge as a person in her own right, she had to free herself of her mother's hold over her.

How does one free herself from the enthrallment of her dead? A lost love is enthralling, it seems, when he or she links us to the other world, when we associate him or her with the unknown, with the mystery that fills the mind with wonder. What keeps us from accepting the loss of the other and releasing his or her image is our fear of the unknown: grieving the loss through means entering the other world. In her everyday life, Woolf professed no religion. But she said that her periods of insanity were a "substitute for religion" and *To the Lighthouse* depicts a journey into the other world. Mrs. Ramsay, the likeness of Woolf's mother, is a numinous figure: she carries the "torch of her beauty"[63] wherever she goes and men feel, in their admiration for her, a reverence for all women. But it is Lily Briscoe, the spinsterish young woman who paints, who senses the otherworldly aspect of Mrs. Ramsay's magnetism. Sitting on the floor, with her arms around the older woman's knees, Lily imagines how "in the chambers of the mind and heart of the woman who was, physically, touching her, were stood, like the treasures in the tomb of kings, tablets bearing sacred inscriptions."[64] Woolf knew she had turned a corner in her life by writing *To the Lighthouse*. Once you have passed over into the other world, your numinous dead are no longer enthralling.

Can it be, then, that the crying child in modern women's psyches is crying for the other world? When our hearts bear an insatiable ache for a time and place, for a loved one who is gone, is it because an other-worldly gleam attaches to the memory? Woolf's mother, according to the author's portrait of her, was a woman who passed effortlessly in and out of the other world. In one of Lily's arguments with Mrs. Ramsay over marriage as the "universal law," the younger woman puts her head down to "laugh and laugh . . . at the thought of Mrs. Ramsay presiding with immutable calm over destinies which she completely failed to understand." When she looks up, the older woman is rapt in contemplation: "there was Mrs. Ramsay, unwitting entirely what had caused her laughter, still presiding, but now with every trace of willfulness abolished, and in its stead, something clear as the space which the clouds at last uncover—the little space of sky which sleeps beside the moon."[65] As a Demeter figure, Mrs. Ramsay possesses the wisdom the goddess acquires when she withdraws into her temple: the knowledge, we could say, of herself as unconditioned. Woolf depicts Mrs. Ramsay as making contact with the unconditioned as a means of spiritual refreshment. Putting the children's toys away after they have all gone to sleep, she reflects:

> now she need not think about anybody. She could be herself, by herself. And that was what she often felt the need of—to think; well, not even to think. To be silent; to be alone. All the being and the doing, expansive, glittering, vocal, evaporated; and one shrunk, with a sense of solemnity, to being oneself, a wedge-shaped core of darkness, something invisible to others. This core of darkness could go anywhere, for no one saw it. They could not stop it, she thought, exulting. There was freedom, there was peace, there was, most welcome of all, a summoning together, a resting on a platform of stability. Not as oneself did one find rest ever, in her experience (she accomplished here something dexterous with her needles) but as a wedge of darkness. Losing personality, one lost the fret, the hurry, the stir, and there rose to her lips always some exclamation of triumph over life when things came together in this peace, this rest, this eternity.[66]

The climax of the first part of *To the Lighthouse* is the dinner party scene in which Mrs. Ramsay creates a timeless moment for her family and guests. All day she has been their point of reference. Sitting in the window with her son James, she was the object of attention of Lily Briscoe who was painting her portrait, Mr. Bankes who interrupted his conversation with Lily to gaze on her in speechless rapture, and Mr. Ramsay, who turned to her for consolation when his thoughts became too melancholy. While they gazed upon her, she would raise her eyes to look, from time to time, at the lighthouse in the harbor. As the dinner begins and Mrs. Ramsay is ladling out soup, the guests sit separate and "nothing [has] merged." Mrs. Ramsay is tired, but she gives herself a "little shake" and begins "the effort of merging and flowing and creating" that transforms the dinner party into one of those sublime experiences that is a window on eternity:

Now all the candles were lit up and the faces on both sides of the table were brought nearer by the candlelight and composed, as they had not been in the twilight, into a party round a table, for the night was now shut off by panes of glass, which, far from giving any accurate view of the outside world, rippled it so strangely that here, inside the room, seemed to be order and dry land; there, outside, a reflection in which all things wavered and vanished, waterily. . . . Some change at once went through them all as if this had really happened, and they were all conscious of making a party together in a hollow, on an island; had their common cause against that fluidity out there.[67]

The "fluidity" which Mrs. Ramsay holds at bay with her gift for "making of the moment something permanent"[68] seems to triumph in Part Two of the book. "Time Passes" is a mournful interlude which portrays the changes wrought in the Ramsay household by ten years' passage of time. Mrs. Ramsay herself dies suddenly one winter. The First World War begins and Andrew Ramsay—the oldest boy—is blown up in France. Prue Ramsay, a beauty like her mother, is given in marriage and dies a year later from complications connected with childbirth. During all these years, the Ramsays' house in the Hebrides is closed up. The omniscient narrator describes the passage of time here in terms of the gradual invasion of nature: swallows nesting in the drawing room; thistles thrusting themselves between the tiles in the larder. Alternating with the descriptive passages is the account of a lonely walker on the beach who asks himself as he gazes out to the horizon the metaphysical questions that express our fear that the passage of time is all there is.

Did Nature supplement what man advanced? Did she complete what he began? With equal complacence she saw his misery, his meanness, and his torture. That dream, of sharing, completing, of finding in solitude on the beach an answer was then but a reflection in a mirror, and the mirror itself was but the surface glassiness which forms in quiescence when the nobler powers sleep beneath?[69]

The question that haunts us when time puts distance between us and a magical period in the past is how do I know that I didn't imagine that glimpse of the other world? How do I know that my memory of the other is not an illusion?

When someone has lost the person who connected her to the other world, she has the sense of the passage of time as empty. The time she spent with the other was lit with meaning, while the time since then seems like an aimless sequence of months and years. The attempt to impose meaning on your life always fails: a willed marriage comes apart; a work that is forced is still-born. But where is a glimmer of meaning to be found? Where is the spark that will enkindle your heart the way the presence of the other did? When the world that is familiar to you is lifeless, when there is nothing green and growing, there is still the other world. And when you shift your gaze from the past to the mind's horizon, you realize there is one thing about the other world that you have always known—its irresistible attraction. You could always be pulled away from a lover or a child or even the wondrous person who mediated the unknown for you by the prospect of your own encounter with it. You also know—you have always known— the vehicle for your encounter, be it writing or painting or some other spirit-filled activity. You have always regarded your spirit-filled activity—writing, let us say—as dangerous. Plato said that to philosophize is to learn to die and you know that your writing will exact a kind of death as the price of your passage to the other world. Mid-life desperation, however, can make a woman fearless. When Lily Briscoe returns to the house in the Hebrides with what is left of the Ramsay family ten years after the summer that glows in her memory, the first thing she does is resolve to finish the painting of Mrs. Ramsay begun ten years earlier.

The instant that you pick up brush or pen everything that is incidental in your life falls away and your essential self is revealed. Writing or painting or any attempt to respond to the claim of the other world on one's mind and heart calls forth one's spiritual being. But in the moment of passage, between the mind's vision and the words on the page or the paint on the canvas, the inner child can interpose herself and block the emergence. "It was in the moment's flight between the picture and her canvas," Lily Briscoe reflects, "that the demons set on her who often brought her to the verge of tears and made this passage from conception to work as dreadful as any down a dark passage for a child."[70] Turning away from the human circle and facing the unknown evokes one's primordial fear of aloneness, for aloneness is death to the person who has always identified with the human circle. Feeling the child's dread, it was all Lily could do, in times past, to keep from "fling[ing] herself . . . at Mrs. Ramsay's knee and say[ing] 'I'm in love with you.'"[71] How much easier it is to worship someone, to be "just a piece of cherished flesh," as Etty Hillesum says,[72] in the arms of another than to be spirit. Yet the mind has such a definite sense of the riches in the other world that it gives the heart no peace until it has consented to the journey. "There was something," Lily remembers as she sets up her easel, "which had stayed in her mind [all these years], which had tied a knot in her mind so that, at odds and ends of time, involuntarily, as she walked along the Brompton Road, as she brushed her hair, she found herself painting that picture, passing her eye over it, and untying the knot in her imagination."[73]

When a woman suffers the child's dread instead of succumbing to it, she is bracing herself for the ordeal of artistic creation. The human spirit versus the unknown—was there ever a struggle more demanding, more purifying in the way that it forces us to rely solely on the heart, the heart apart from the instincts—the heart bereft of all the supports that sustain us in the human circle? For it is the heart that receives messages from the unknown; the mind's job is to decode them. While Woolf was working on *Mrs. Dalloway*, she had an experience that illustrates how intense an encounter with the unknown can be. "It was a wet, windy night, and as I walked back across the field I said, Now I am meeting it; now the old devil has once more got his spine through the waves . . . . And such was the strength of my feeling that I became physically rigid. Reality, so I thought, was unveiled."[74] In the scenes in *Mrs. Dalloway* portraying Septimus Warren Smith's madness, we get an idea of what it can be like to face the unknown without the will for artistic creation, when the self is not braced but broken and the inability to communicate what one perceives makes it seem that one is trapped beyond the human circle forever.

> He started up in terror. What did he see? The plate of bananas on the sideboard. Nobody was there. . . . That was it: to be alone forever. That was the doom pronounced in Milan when he came into the room and saw them cutting out buckram shapes with their scissors; to be alone forever. . . . He was alone with the sideboard and the bananas.[75]

We need to brace ourselves, in the process of artistic creation, so that the unknown can work its power on us and awaken spiritual desire. Spirit's desire for the unknown can become a strong current and one's art

> an exacting form of intercourse . . . the mass loomed before [Lily]; it protruded; she felt it pressing on her eyeballs. Then, as if some juice necessary for the lubrication of her faculties were spontaneously squirted, she began precariously dipping among the blues and umbers, moving her brush hither and thither, but now it was heavier and went slower, as if it had fallen in with some rhythm which was dictated to her (she kept looking at the hedge, at the canvas) by what she saw, so that while her hand quivered with life, this rhythm was strong enough to bear her along with it, on its current.[76]

The secret of the artist, which she may not grasp fully herself, is that her real passion is for the unknown. Lily Briscoe has never had a lover. She shrinks from the touch of men. It was only Mrs. Ramsay who could arouse feeling in her and the death of Mrs. Ramsay has caused her to lock that feeling away. When we bury the image of the person who connected us to the other world, we bury our spiritual passion along with it. Giving full expression to our spiritual passion involves releasing that image. Lily's thoughts turn to Mrs. Ramsay while she is painting.

> But what a power was in the human soul! she thought. That woman sitting there writing under the rock resolved everything into simplicity, made these angers, irritations, fall off like old rags; she brought together this and that and then this, and so made out of that miserable silliness and spite . . . something . . . [that] stayed in the mind affecting one almost like a work of art.[77]

The No to death that kept Demeter from relenting to the will of Zeus is the knot in one's heart around one's sacred image. The irony is that one loved the other for his or her freedom of spirit—the ability to pass smoothly in and out of the other world—but this attachment to the other is trammeling one's own spirit. As we have said, the real issue is fear. A person is afraid to unlock her heart, afraid to release the image because then she will really be alone. The price of freedom of spirit, it seems, is aloneness. If we can't overcome our fear directly, we can be tricked into overcoming it. The effort of concentration required by writing or painting steadies us as we enter uncharted regions of the self. "And Lily, painting steadily, felt as if a door had opened, and one went in and stood gazing silently about in a high cathedral-like place, very dark, very solemn."[78] Art can be the vehicle to what we have called the still point—the point in the self where one touches on eternity and the things of one's life become transparent. "The great revelation had never come," Lily reflects. "The great revelation perhaps never did come. Instead, there were little daily miracles, illuminations, matches struck unexpectedly in the dark."[79] We can imagine that Virginia Woolf came into touch with the still point in herself through her writing. We can say that *To the Lighthouse* was a turning point for her because it indicates that she became centered at the still point.

In 1923, when she was working on *Mrs. Dalloway*, Woolf had made a diary entry that reflected her need for inner freedom. She remembers how, as a young woman, after Lytton Strachey had withdrawn his proposal of marriage, she said to herself

> never pretend that the things you haven't got are not worth having . . . children, for instance . . . one must . . . like things for themselves; or rather, rid them of their bearing upon one's personal life. One must throw that aside; and venture on to the things that exist independently of oneself.[80]

She goes on to lament that living with Leonard, she needn't make the effort to transcend egocentrism; she fears that she has became "cowardly and self-indulgent."[81] One only transcends egocentrism by becoming centered at the still point. Freedom of spirit is being able to relate to others in light of the eternal—ascribing to them the same foundation in mystery that I discover in myself at the still point. Until I acknowledge the mystery of the other, our relationship is flat; the other might as well be a thing made solely for me. The acknowledgment of mystery gives our relationship depth: there is resonance instead of nothingness across the distance between us. Freedom of spirit is the ability to resonate with the other—to feel in one's heart the wonder of the other's being. The heart that is clutching a sacred image is blocked in its relationships. Writing or painting or any spirit-filled activity makes us feel the pain of that blockage.

One of the great gifts of art is that it makes the impossible possible and induces a kind of faith in the artist. The writer finds herself expressing what she thought was inexpressible; the painter sees before her on the canvas a miracle of line and color. When you are practicing your art, you have the marvelous sense that anything can happen—and you shed your usual inhibitions. A child who loses a beloved parent can learn from that experience that what she wants most in life she can't have and she will adjust her expectations accordingly. It will never occur to her that there might be a point in expressing her unrequited longing; she will accept it as the affective context of the rest of her life. But when she takes up pen or brush, she becomes a different person. Spiritual desire rises up in her as if there were a God, as if her unrequited longing might have a term different from the one she had imagined. Why should she cry out the name of her lost love to the void? Desire gives her the wild thought that there will be a disclosure, that the human heart can penetrate the mystery of death. Most of the time Lily Briscoe is "like most middle-aged people, cautious, furtive, with wrinkles between the eyes and a look of perpetual apprehension."[82] But as she paints the picture of Mrs. Ramsay, the broken-hearted child in her cries out her anguish:

> how could one express in words these emotions of the body? Express that emptiness there? (She was looking at the drawing-room steps; they looked extraordinarily empty.) It was one's body feeling, not one's mind. The physical sensations that went with the bare look of the step had become suddenly extremely unpleasant. To want and not to have, sent all up her body a hardness, a hollowness, a strain. And then to want and not to have—to want and want—how that wrung the heart and wrung it again and again! Oh, Mrs. Ramsay! she called out silently.[83]

At the climax of the Eleusinian mysteries, at which the story of Demeter and Persephone was enacted, the high priest descended into a dark place and simulated intercourse with the great goddess. He reappeared to the crowd holding up an ear of corn and announcing "the goddess has given birth to Brimo"[84]—the divine child. There is a point in our intercourse with the unknown at which the crying child is revealed as the divine child. It is the point when we cry out our anguish to the unknown. The cry is the yes to death that releases the sacred image; that you make it to the unknown indicates your willingness to pass over into the other world. Once we release the image, there is only the self and its desire for the unknown. Willingness allows desire to come to term in the other world. It is the divine child in us that is willing to pass over, that trusts the unknown. Right after Lily calls out Mrs. Ramsay's name, she is seized by the conviction that expressing her heart's anguish to the unknown will elicit a response.

> For one moment, she felt that if they both [she and Mr. Carmichael] got up, here, now, on the lawn, and demanded an explanation, why was it so short, why was it so inexplicable, said it with violence, as two fully equipped human beings from whom nothing should be hidden might speak, then, beauty would roll itself up, the space would fill; those empty flourishes would form into shape; if they shouted loud enough Mrs. Ramsay would return. "Mrs. Ramsay!" she said aloud. "Mrs. Ramsay!" The tears ran down her face.[85]

The birth of the divine child is the emergence into consciousness of our connection to the unknown, our ultimate foundation in mystery. This is the still point—a place of emptiness and freedom. That we dwell in the eternal, that our only resting place is God—this is the wisdom of the divine child. Letting go of the sacred image and saying yes to the eternal heals the broken circle of the self and when the circle of the self comes together, it is transparent, as Kierkegaard says, to its transcendent ground. I let go of my sacred image when I am willing to be revealed as what I am eternally; my dread of the unknown was my resistance to that disclosure. The mystery that is penetrated when I say yes to death and open my heart to the unknown is thus the mystery of myself. And the self, willing to be itself—again quoting Kierkegaard—willing to relate to the unknown through itself without the mediation of any other—is a sublime mystery. To penetrate the mystery of myself is not to dispel it but rather to experience it, to know the mystery from within, from a deep and satisfying enjoyment of it. All my life, I realize when the divine child emerges, I have lived outside myself—alienated from the wonder of my own being. Virginia Woolf always felt inferior, we know, to her mother and sister and other "real women."[86] Being a writer did not compensate, in her mind, for her lack of children. But when Lily Briscoe cries out Mrs. Ramsay's name and "steps off her strip of board into the waters of annihilation"[87] it is hard not to imagine an experience of rebirth on Woolf's part. When Lily has a vision of Mrs. Ramsay, just as she is completing her painting, we can't help but think that the rent in Woolf's soul due to the loss of her mother became healed.

What causes interior division—the split between the child and the mother in a woman's psyche—is unwillingness. How many women suffer this split because they are unwilling to live an unmediated existence, they are unwilling to relate to the unknown on their own when they lose the person who mediated it for them. Unwillingness can express itself in the "search for the sunlit meadow" that we found in Joan Didion, the denial of one's aloneness by succumbing to nostalgia—attempting to re-enact golden moments from one's past instead of facing the reality of the present. Unwillingness also expresses itself as defiance. The new life Felicitas creates for herself with its web of willed relationships, in *The Company of Women*, expresses her passionate rejection of the solitary existence of her friend Father Cyprian and his solitary God. But this rejection reflects, as Mary Gordon's subsequent book *Men and Angels* suggests, her unwillingness to feel the loneliness and sense of abandonment that had sent the younger Felicitas into a deep depression. Virginia Woolf seems to have envisioned another way of resolving the split between the crying child and the mature woman in her before she wrote *To the Lighthouse*. *Night and Day* proposes the solution of sharing one's aloneness with another person as if the touch of another on the level of one's deep aloneness might be healing. But in

Mrs. Dalloway, the radical disjunction between the society woman—representing the self one shows to others—and the madman—representing one's inner, solitary self—suggests that the solution Woolf proposed, and probably tried in her own life, had failed.

It is only when we are willing to be that solitary self, when we cross over from the familiar world of mediated existence to the other world of the unmediated that we experience healing. Spirit in me wants to live in both worlds; I am half the person I am meant to be until I cross over. Joining the two worlds through my yes to the unknown is like coming to rest, as Woolf says, on a "platform of stability." Whereas previously I was anxious and insecure, questioning my self-worth, now my self-possession seems unassailable and my self-doubts like so many gnats that irritate without causing harm. "It would be hung in the attic," Lily Briscoe thinks to herself as she surveys her almost completed painting, "it would be destroyed. But what did that matter?"[88] The affirmation that you always sought from without, particularly from your mediating figure, now comes from within. Suddenly, the mediating figure is an equal. Lily has a vision of Mrs. Ramsay because she has made the journey to the other world; her spirit is as free to pass back and forth from the temporal to the eternal as Mrs. Ramsay's was. All those years, we realize, between Lily's first encounter with Mrs. Ramsay—when she fell in love with her—and her reunion with Mrs. Ramsay in the eternal dimension, Lily was poised on the brink of the other world. She was waiting to overcome her fear.

That is the experience of the "deadly clear path" when the next thing is death, when the next thing is to let go of your life, your familiar life in the human circle—and you are afraid to let go. There is a time for death to be a companion, a time to let the awareness of death temper the spirit. Think of all that Demeter learns on her sojourn among the "cities of men." But a woman must never lose herself in the struggle against death. When the children are born and cared for, when the tasks she sets herself are accomplished, she must hearken to the crying child in her that longs for the other world. For some women, the transition is easy: they have never totally identified with their roles in the human circle. For others, the transition amounts to an identity crisis: instead of relating consciously to the life-force, they have surrendered themselves to it and their sense of themselves as powerful precludes acknowledgment of the crying child. Once one has acknowledged her, one's struggle is no longer with death, but with God, with the un-known. This is one's true identity: a woman who longs for and fears a relationship with God. Again and again, you may come to the point of releasing your sacred image, of crossing over into the world that you glimpsed through the other. But fear of God, fear of the unknown holds you back. A woman comes through the impasse, as Lily Briscoe discovers, when she gives voice to the crying child, when she expresses her anguish to the unknown. The Living God, Sri Ramakrishnan says, is like a mother who is waiting for her children to put down their toys and start to cry.

With the emergence of the divine child, we have come upon that which, according to Simone Weil, is "sacred in human beings," that "something . . . deep in the heart . . . that goes on indomitably expecting, in the teeth of all crimes ex-perienced, suffered, and witnessed, that good and not evil will be done to [us]." The divine child corresponds to our partici-pation in mystery; with that awareness we have the sense that the holy mystery is our destiny, as if we were being carried by a deep current into the future. The heart expands with the realization that death in a sense is behind you, that the road ahead does not end in a dark tunnel, but opens out to infinity. You have come through the dark tunnel and time, as Plato says, seems like a changing image of eternity. It must be our awareness of the interconnectedness of time and eternity, at this point, that gives us that expectation of goodness to which Simone Weil refers. Whatever happens, we know, we are car-ried by the eternal, by God. Therefore God can be found in whatever happens. I can find peace in the midst of conflict, rest in my restless striving to accomplish something with my life. And like Lily Briscoe, who knows that her painting will be hung in the attic, I have the lightsome sense that the results of my striving are not the point. "The world and time," Thomas Merton says,

> are the dance of the Lord in emptiness. The silence of the spheres is the music of a wedding feast. The more we persist in misunderstanding the phenomena of life, the more we analyze them out into strange finalities and complex purposes of our own, the more we involve ourselves in sadness, absurdity, and despair. But it does not matter much, because no despair of ours can alter the reality of things or stain the joy of the cosmic dance which is always there.[89]

The emergence of the divine child is the end of a journey. Lily Briscoe finishes her painting just as Mr. Ramsay and two of the children disembark at the lighthouse.

FIVE

The Woman and God:
Etty Hillesum

There are two ways a woman can go when she makes the discovery of her divine child: she can return to the human circle where her new-found sense of herself will be a light that beckons other women to make the same discovery or she can stay on the boundary of the human circle waiting for another glimpse of God. Even if she returns to the human circle, if she takes up her former relationships, her previous projects, a longing in her soul has been enkindled such that the human circle as she has known it will never seem like home again. We can imagine the woman in Camus's story "The Adulterous Wife" going back to her husband. In the story, she leaves him one night to go out in the desert where she has intercourse with the night sky. How does the woman, we wonder, now receive her husband's embrace? How does she give herself to him when the night sky beckons and stirs up her soul's wildness? This is the dilemma she seems to face: if she returns to the human circle, she risks losing touch with her wild soul, but if she abandons herself to her soul's longing, she risks losing touch with all that she values in the human circle. "Once one has seen God, what is the remedy?"[1] We remember this plaintive line from Sylvia Plath, written just two weeks before she committed suicide. Already alienated from the human circle, Plath seems to have regarded her mystical experiences as another sign of her alienation, as if the knowledge of God marked her out for a solitary life. But what if you feel a connection to the human circle? What if the life-force surges up continually in you demanding your involvement in others' lives and community projects? Can a woman have both? Can she love the God of the shining sky without denying her heart's native attachments?

For someone to succeed in bringing the life-force and the God of the shining sky together would be to achieve the synthesis that Western civilization since the rise of patriarchal religion has by and large failed to realize. From the time that the Kurgan peoples invaded the centers of goddess religion, destroying the temples and much of the culture, the power of the life-force has been feared and despised. Especially in its sexual expression, it has been regarded as dangerous, liable to subvert one's allegiance to patriarchal authority. The story of humankind's fall in Genesis portrays the serpent—symbol of the life-force from the goddess tradition—as the cause of Adam and Eve's violation of the divine prohibition. The woman who has encountered the Living God, who has overcome her fear of darkness and solitude and discovered the transcendent orientation of her soul, knows that God is not identical to patriarchal authority. Instead of despising the life-force, she values it as the sign of her soul's good health, as an indicator of her natural craving for all the things of life. But the transcendent orientation of her soul and her natural craving seem to pull her in opposite directions. Is there, she wonders, a way to unify the desires that threaten to divide her?

The woman we are imagining has had a glimpse of unity. Overcoming her fear and saying yes to her desire for the Unknown was a moment of "passing over," as the theologian John Dunne puts it,[2] into the divine life. The heart's rapture, which she experienced in solitude, is a taste of eternal life. Giving birth to her divine child is the realization that she is destined for eternal life. In the eternal dimension, there is no separation between self and God: transcendent love fills the heart to overflowing. Even when she comes back to herself, as we say, to her life in time, unity is signified by the way that trust has replaced fear in her relationship with God. If she only looks in one direction—away from the human circle—at this point, it can seem that the purpose of life is simply to die, to pass over permanently into the divine life. Life in time, from this perspective, is essentially a waiting-to-die and the life-force, which impels us toward people and projects, something to be resisted. But if she turns toward the human circle, relying on her sense of unity, the purpose of her life in time seems more mysterious. The people in her life seem to hold something for her. Can we experience the eternal not only beyond the human circle but also within it? Does the life-force point the way to luminous encounters?

What we are envisioning is an integrated experience of the life-force: a desire for the other that is a desire for communion rather than possession, an engagement in work that is self-transcending instead of self-seeking. But is such a vision realistic? The portrayal of the life-force as a serpent is telling: its immense power springs from the non-human part of the psyche which is indifferent to the distinction between good and evil. Let us say that the woman we are imagining comes to see that her life has been determined, more than she has realized, by the power of the life-force. As a young woman, she abandoned herself willingly to sexual desire; as a mature woman, she let the maternal instinct rule her life. She sees the dark as well as the bright aspect of the power of the life-force: the jealousy that went with sexual desire, the ruthlessness of the maternal instinct. But jealousy to a betrayed woman and ruthlessness to a mother whose child is in danger seem as natural, she knows, as breathing. If it is not unrealistic to envision an integration of the life-force, we must realize from the outset that what we are contemplating involves nothing less than a transformation of our instinctual responses.

The serpent and the God of the shining sky—why should we think that the opposition between the two might be overcome? There are images from the Christian tradition which suggest that the opposition is inherent and that the right way to relate to the life-force is to repress it. I am thinking of statues from my Catholic childhood which depicted Mary the mother of Jesus wearing a crown of stars and standing on a globe of the world with her feet crushing a serpent's head. These statues reinforced the view that reality was divided into the spiritual and the non-spiritual with the non-spiritual existing to be limited, controlled, and ultimately defeated by the spiritual. But to know the true God of the shining sky, to carry in your heart a seed of pure love planted in the moment of encounter, is to know that the divine life transcends the nature-spirit dualism we normally experience. The Living God is *not* opposed to our desire for life. Patriarchal traditions which set God over against nature reflect a lack of knowledge of the divine life. The opposition which we perceive between God and the life-force can only come from our side: *from our inability to participate fully in the divine life*.

The story of Eros and Psyche, as we have interpreted it, describes an overcoming of the split between divine love—or our participation in divine love—and instinctual love in our souls. At the beginning of her journey, Psyche is open to transcendent love—that is the significance of her marriage to the "heavenly bridegroom" before her journey begins—but it is only through the course of her journey that she becomes open to the divine in the non-spiritual part of her soul. When Psyche is taken up into heaven at the end of the story, what is signified is a whole human being—nature as well as spirit—becoming capable of participating in the divine life. Etty Hillesum is a twentieth-century female author whose spiritual journey seems to have been remarkably like Psyche's. The diary she kept for a year and a half during the Nazi occupation of Amsterdam reflects a progression from transcending the life-force through her discovery of the divine life to integrating the life-force through participation in the divine life. As a Jew, Etty realizes that she lives under the threat of deportation and murder almost from the beginning of her journal entries. Her participation in the divine life is so complete by the end of the book that we find her refusing an exemption that might have saved her from the fate of her people in order to be a healing presence in the death camps. From reading her diary, which concludes on the eve of her final return to Westerbork, the transport camp where she worked for a year before being sent to Auschwitz, one is left with the impression of a person brimming with life. By tracing her journey, we should be able to see how any modern woman might integrate the life-force with the divine life.

I. Transcending the Life-force through Discovery of the Divine Life

DISTINGUISHING BETWEEN FANTASIES AND THE DESIRE OF THE HEART

From the time Etty met Julius Spier, the psychochiriologist or palm reader who became her mentor and great friend, many of her reflections centered on him and her relationship with him. Spier seems to have been the catalyst for her beginning a diary. A sophisticated woman who comes up against a man who seems to be able to read her soul is thrown off balance. When a woman is accustomed to getting what she wants in relationships, it is disconcerting to meet someone whom she knows she can't manipulate. It is also enthralling. Etty hesitated, she reports in her diary, taking the time to observe him from a distance at a public lecture, but eventually she "yielded [herself] unreservedly to him."[3] Her diary seems to be an attempt to restore her equilibrium—to go deep within herself so as to be able to return his knowing gaze. She describes her effort as a search for what is "truly essential" in her which seems to be "locked away." "Deep down," she writes, "something like a tightly wound ball of twine binds me relentlessly" so that "at times, I am nothing more or less than a miserable, frightened creature."[4]

What threatened to impede Etty's process of self-discovery right from the start would seem to have been Spier himself. She describes him as "A 54-year-old in whom the struggle between the spirit and the flesh is still in full cry."[5] Sessions with his clients involved wrestling matches and, in Etty's case, other physical contact. At one point, when he "lay groaning on top of" her, she thought to herself, "a funny way of treating patients you have, you get your pleasure out of it and you get paid for it as well."[6] After a few sessions, Etty's erotic desires were focused on Spier. Her early journal entries describe fantasies she has about being his one and only beloved. Spier had a fiancée, a young woman named Hertha, who was living in London, and Etty confesses to being envious of her. She describes how she had gone to one therapy session dressed seductively in a kind of rapturous anticipation of love-making with Spier. What happened, though, was "an immediate and mighty collision of [her] extravagant fantasy life with the sober reality: an embarrassed and sweating man tucking a crumpled shirt into his trousers when it was all over."[7]

When a person awakens a woman's soul—gives her the sense of a mysterious life that she, too, could live if only she went deep enough within herself—it is inevitable that that person will stir up the life-force and become the dominant figure of her fantasy life. Let's say the other person is a man. She will be sure to encounter his image in her dreams and, like Etty, she will live in rapturous anticipation of her meetings with him. Instinctively, we crave life and in this case our instincts impel us toward the other as to a new source of life. Even if Spier had never touched Etty physically, she would still have come under his spell. In a convoluted passage where she is trying to sort through her feelings for him, Etty realizes that her desire for Spier was present before he had aroused her sexually:

And when I sat facing him again and fell silent, I was moved perhaps just as I used to be by a walk through beautiful scenery. I wanted to "own" him. I wanted him to be part of me. True, I did not long for him as one longs for a man, he had not yet moved me sexually, and though I never felt quite relaxed with him he had touched me to the very depths of my being, and that was more important. And so I wanted to own him and I hated all those women of whom he had spoken to me.[8]

The passage just quoted reminds us again of Simone Weil's statement (which reflects a negative view of the life-force) that the great tragedy of human life is that looking and eating are two different operations. We love the beautiful person on whom we have turned our gaze—he awakens a deep yearning in us—but then fantasies of possession render our desire impure. If we act on those fantasies by attempting to possess the other sexually, we can lose sight of the deep yearning that was our initial response to him. "First we feel and then we fall,"[9] James Joyce says, as if the transition from pure desire to games of sexual conquest were inevitable, as if the soul-stirring occasioned by the other were necessarily eclipsed. According to Simone Weil, the only way to keep from "falling" is to wrench one's desire away from its object—to turn away from the beautiful person and consent to love "in the void," i.e., refusing to allow fantasies of possession to fill one's mind.[10] Etty's method of purification was less drastic. She thought about renouncing all contact with Spier, but rejected the idea. Instead, she focused her energy on understanding her feelings, trusting that her deepest feelings would provide direction for the spiritual growth she was seeking.

We need to underscore the importance of Etty's choice of spiritual method. It places her squarely within the goddess tradition, which teaches women to seek illumination by turning inward, by getting in touch with what is deepest in ourselves, instead of conforming to an abstract ideal of perfection. The latter approach, it would seem, by rejecting the life-force, implies a fundamental distrust of the self, of the feeling, desiring, embodied self which creates the images that channel what Simone Weil calls our vital energy. But why should we deny our fantasies? What is there to fear in our desires? To be sure, enthrallment by the object of our desires is a real temptation. It is easy to imagine that many a spiritual journey has been sidetracked indefinitely by the seeker's abandonment to the play of desire. Etty's diary records numerous instances of her struggling with this temptation. One of her first entries reports, "Just the sound of his voice over the telephone tonight was enough to make my body betray me. But I swore like a navvy, telling myself that I was no longer a hysterical teenager. And I suddenly understood those monks who flagellate themselves to tame their sinful flesh."[11] But if we do not begin with our real feelings and desires, the spiritual journey is not real. It remains a beautiful idea that never takes root in our hearts.

When Etty examined her feelings, what she found was that she was not really in love with Spier: "As I was cycling about in the cold, I suddenly thought: perhaps I am making everything much too complicated because I don't want to face the sober facts. I am not really in love with him."[12] This is one of the hardest admissions a woman can make. I remember coming to the point in my own life where I had to determine whether or not to commit myself to a relationship. I was standing in the kitchen of the little house I was renting with two other women and I knew that if I waited there, my heart would speak. My fantasies had already made the man my husband; he was just the kind of person I could imagine as a life partner. I didn't wait in the kitchen that day because I couldn't face the consequences of what I guessed to be true—that however alluring my boyfriend's image, my heart wasn't in a relationship with him. "Woman's main interest is the ideal man," Etty writes, "man's is the world at large. Can woman shift her focus without losing her own power, without doing violence to her real being?"[13] At the age of twenty-two, I was sure the answer was no.

The shift from dismissing your fantasies as a temptation to trying to understand them allows a person to make the distinction between fantasies and the desire of one's heart. When the heart goes unprobed, it is easy to think that intense attraction and the corresponding glittering images indicate that the heart has been captured by the other. But when you "descend with your mind into your heart" as the monastic saying goes, you begin to differentiate between intensity of feeling and depth of feeling. Intense attraction may turn out to have very deep roots or it may be discontinuous with what is deepest in your heart. When Etty wrote that she was not in love with Spier, she was saying that the depth of feeling he awakened in her was something altogether different from her erotic fantasies about him—that it did not point in the direction of a romantic relationship. In one passage, she admits that physical intimacy with him makes her melancholy:

> But a moment later his body was suddenly on mine and I was in his arms, and then I suddenly felt sad and lonely. He kissed my thighs and I grew lonelier still. He said, "That was lovely," and I went home with a leaden, sad, abandoned feeling.[14]

She supposes that she feels this way because she is unable "to surrender to [their] physical contact with [her] deepest being."[15]

It is a very lonely feeling to be differentiated from your fantasies. It seems as though you've forgotten the movements to a universal dance. We remember Sylvia Plath's poem, "The Disquieting Muses," in which she identifies with the forgotten fairy from Sleeping Beauty because she knows in her heart that she is not the golden girl of her mother's—and her—dreams. But where Plath dreaded individuation, Etty welcomed it. She recognized that until she claimed the deep self that undercuts our fantasies, she would not be whole. She had the fundamental anxiety of the person who knows that something essential to her life is missing. I believe that her friendship with Spier was of inestimable value to Etty as she shifted her focus away from her fantasies. The presence of a real individual is both challenge and support to the rest of us. What Etty found, as she shifted her focus, was that it effected a balance of power between her and Spier. He was no longer the "magical personality" and she the adoring disciple. "And now I feel that I am a match for him," she writes, "that my struggle is balanced against his, that in me, too, both impure and nobler impulses are fighting a mighty battle."[16]

SEEING THROUGH THE FANTASIES

While we can engage in the struggle between our fantasies and the desire of the heart by an effort of will—by acknowledging the heart's resistance to our most cherished fantasies—coming through the struggle requires willingness. The theologian John Dunne, who makes the distinction between will and willingness in his book *The Peace of the Present*, correlates the self of willingness with one's "center of stillness"—Dag Hammarskjöld's term which we have been using to describe the discovery Demeter makes when she withdraws into her temple. Etty's diary records her discovery of her center of stillness after months of inner turmoil and division. Until that point, as much as she knew that she didn't want a relationship with Spier, she was bedeviled by her continuing attachment to the idea. In analyzing her problem, she sees quite readily that the real obstacle is her unwillingness to emerge as an individual—to be who she is as she is and not as she imagines herself to be in her extravagant fantasies. "I am still ashamed of myself, afraid to let myself go, to let things pour out of me; I am dreadfully inhibited, and that is because I have not yet learned to accept myself as I am."[17]

Unwillingness to be the person you are means that wherever you go, you meet your self-reflection. The image of yourself performing brilliantly or looking glamorous or devoting yourself to an illustrious partner haunts and frustrates your actual efforts to be true to yourself—to discern and follow the desire of your heart. There are comical passages in Etty's diary where she describes her obsession with her self-image:

> And for goodness' sake, stop looking at yourself in the mirror, Etty, you fool. . . . The time I spend in front of the mirror because I am suddenly caught by a funny or fascinating or interesting expression on this really not particularly pretty face of mine, could surely be spent on better things. It annoys me terribly, all this peering at myself. Sometimes I do find that I am looking pretty, but that's largely because of the dim lighting in the bathroom, and at such moments I can't tear myself away from my likeness and pull faces at myself in the glass, hold my head at all sorts of angles before my enraptured gaze, and then my favourite fantasy is that I'm seated in a large hall behind a table and facing a large company, all of whom keep looking at me and find me beautiful.[18]

When a person is only conscious of her self-image and out of touch with her deep self, she can feel that she is cut off from the world, trapped in a bell jar, to use Sylvia Plath's metaphor. When Etty complains of feeling depressed and "plugged up" inside, it is precisely this lack of connection that she seems to be experiencing. Until she had her breakthrough, she was frequently depressed. Visits to her parents' house, for example, where she had to interact with her "materialistic" mother, left her feeling as if "every bit of energy were being sucked out" of her.[19]

When a change in circumstances causes a decrease in one's supply of vital energy, the instinctive response is to seek compensation—to do or imagine whatever causes a return of the life-force, an upsurge of the desire to engage with the things of life. When Etty was depressed, she found herself more susceptible than ever to fantasies of being Spier's one true love. She berates herself for imagining him saying to her "You alone forever more," and allowing that to fan the flame of her erotic desires.[20] She also developed an eating disorder.

Numerous times she confesses to ruining her digestion by eating too much. She interprets both tendencies as indicating a kind of metaphysical greed or "hunger for the absolute," which she sees as having been overpowering at earlier points in her life. About an affair that she had at eighteen, which she regards as a tragic episode, she writes, "I'm only just beginning to understand all that passion in my relationship with Max. It was sheer desperation because I knew he was unobtainable and that very knowledge spurred me on, no doubt because I tried to reach him in the wrong way. Too absolute. And the absolute does not exist."[21]

What Etty is saying in the above passage is that her unwillingness to accept the reality of her lover's indifference inflamed to an even greater degree her passion for him—to the point, she tells us later, that it became destructive. When they parted, she was utterly despairing. Now that she understands the root of her grandiose passions, she is able to experience them without being overwhelmed. But the strain of feeling them without allowing herself to give in to them was a frequent source of irritation. From time to time, it gave rise to feelings of antipathy towards Spier, who seemed to be able to live with the tension much more serenely. One night, when she had come to his apartment with the intention of asking forgiveness for all the "ugly and rebellious thoughts" she had been having about him, she had an outburst instead. She threw her coat, hat, gloves, bag, and notebook across the room. When asked what was the matter, she replied, "Look, I don't feel up to it, I feel like breaking something, so thank your lucky stars that the flower pots on the windowsill aren't smashed to bits."[22]

What keeps a person from caving in under the tension between her "hunger for the absolute" and her true heart's desire? The difficulty is that as long as she is captivated by an illusory absolute, the deeper longing of her heart is not felt—or felt only as the faintest resonance to the idea of that deeper longing. Spier's oft-repeated admonition to Etty to be true to herself was helpful, she reports, but more important was the discipline of keeping a diary. An entry from early on in their relationship reads, "I must make sure I keep up with my writing, that is, with myself, or else things will start to go wrong with me: I shall run the risk of losing my way."[23] We can see in Etty's writing one of those "impossible tasks" of Psyche's which paved the way for the emergence of her divine spark. Writing is simply the process of finding the right words for things. It is "impossible" in that the words don't come by an exercise of will. One must be open to the truth, willing to know the right name for something. Willingness to know the right name for what we are feeling orients us in the direction of our emerging individuality. Identifying what seems to be a great passion as a flight from your individuality discloses the void in which the true heart's desire can be felt.

ENTERING THE VOID

Facing the void is not like facing a new thing in your life; rather, it is admitting into consciousness the darkness that surrounds the things of life. It is an expansion of consciousness to include the darkness. We saw an awareness of the void in Virginia Woolf's description of human relationships; she seemed to be saying that there are inevitably gaps in them which leave the two people feeling alienated and alone. But aloneness is also opportunity. To a person obsessed with her self-image, embracing aloneness can be a way of stepping through the mirror. When you embrace your aloneness—when you enter the void—you feel as though you are joined at the center of yourself, that the chink in your self-relation has been filled. The self of will, John Dunne would say, has become the self of willingness, for the test of willingness in a person who has always known herself through relationships is the ability to walk alone. Etty reports a momentous change in her relationship with Spier that clearly indicates a shift from will to willingness: "It is as if . . . I had finally wrenched myself clear of him, when I had imagined I was perfectly free all along. I felt it deep down inside me then: my life must be completely independent."[24]

This turning point was preceded by a period of introspection in which she gradually came to realize that it was not just Spier but marriage that her heart opposed. For a long time, she had believed that her life's path was to be like that of most women—that eventually she would devote herself to a man. But the more she meditated on the true nature of her relationship with Spier, the more she saw her dream of true love as a way of escaping the reality of our separateness. The diary entries in which she sets forth this view have the stoical quality of a person facing up to an unwelcome truth:

> It is a slow and painful process, this striving after true inner freedom. Growing more and more certain that there is no help or assurance or refuge in others. That the others are just as uncertain and weak and helpless as you are. You are always thrown back on to your own resources. There is nothing else. The rest is make-believe. But that fact has to be recognized over and over again. Especially since you are a woman. For woman always longs to lose herself in another. But that too is a fiction, albeit a beautiful one. There is no matching of lives. At least not for me.[25]

The prospect of a solitary life strikes her as very difficult: "God knows, being alone is hard. For the world is inhospitable. In the past I used to dream of [being with] one person. But it was not to be. And when you reach such painful truths at the age of 27, you sometimes feel quite desperate and lonely and *anxious*. . . ."[26]

Along with her dread of the single life, there was a definite sense of anticipation in Etty. She had just the mixture of feelings, it seems, that a woman has when she is about to give birth. In that case, dread of the coming ordeal constricts your heart, but the expectation of new life gives you courage. When a woman approaches the void with hopefulness, its aspect changes. Instead of a nothingness, the negation of the things of life, it appears as the dark form of being. She begins to see possibilities in aloneness and darkness that were hidden as long as her attention was focused on the human circle. Three months after she met Spier, Etty made a resolution to spend a half-hour every morning in silent meditation. She called it "turning inward" to "listen to [her] inner voice."[27] Even as she was forming the resolution, she envisioned the richness of a deeper life to be discovered: "So let this be the aim of meditation: to turn one's innermost being into a vast empty plain. . . . So that something of 'God' can enter you, and something of 'Love' too."[28]

The diary reveals that Etty brought her interior division into her meditation periods. Her imagination fluctuated, she tells us, between fantasies of herself as a great writer, "drawing herself life-size in colorful, sweeping words"[29] and opposite fantasies of withdrawing to the silence and seclusion of a convent. In her obsession with greatness, we can see her "hunger for the absolute" in a new form; her convent fantasies seem to indicate a desire to be rid of the whole problem of individual selfhood. In meditation, inner conflict becomes intense. The gap between what you are and what you imagine yourself to be is painfully obvious and your resistance to being what you are—as if your heart were a clenched fist—can be excruciating. No wonder Etty had dreams of running away from her life. One diary entry gives expression to a death wish: "When I cycled home yesterday, so unspeakably sad and as heavy as lead inside, and heard an aeroplane overhead, I was suddenly struck by the notion that a bomb might put an end to my life and I felt liberated. It's been happening more often, that feeling that it's easier not to go on."[30]

What kept Etty going were times when her inner chaos quieted and she had an intimation of the pure desire of her heart. After a passage in which she describes the tremendous effort it sometimes takes for her to accomplish basic tasks like "getting up . . . laying the table" and "putting on stockings without holes," we find, "There is a strange little melody in me that sometimes cries out for words."[31] When she turned away from the human circle and the dream of true love that pointed her in the direction of woman's traditional place in it, she could become aware of the desire of her heart as pointing in an altogether different direction. Before, she had known her heart's desire only as something other than the universal dream, only as the source of the resistance she felt to pursuing that dream. But as she became more and more willing to enter the void, more and more willing to walk alone, it could be felt as pure desire. She realized that there is a path she was meant to follow, one on which her heart could sing. We must be simple enough, though, to want nothing more than for our hearts to sing. Etty complains that "through inhibition, lack of self-confidence, laziness, and goodness knows what else, [her] tune remains stifled, haunting [her] from within."[32]

It is in an entry from November 1941, eight months after she began her diary, that we find what we might call Etty's prayer of willingness. Up to this point, she has referred to God infrequently—though an August entry makes it clear that she has experienced the presence of God: "There is a really deep well inside me and in it dwells God. Sometimes I am there too. But more often stones and grit block the well and God is buried beneath. Then he must be dug out again."[33] When you are facing the void, trying to come to grips with aloneness and darkness, there may come a time when you feel your resistant heart unclenching. It seems as though you have entered a clearing after fighting your way through dense underbrush. You are in the holy place of your center of stillness where you are aware of the presence of God. It may be that Etty's experience of the presence of God during this period was a frequent occurrence even though she does not say so. Because of their intimate nature, she tells us, she found it hard to find words for her prayer experiences. For a long time, she was embarrassed by the very act of kneeling. "The girl who could not kneel," she calls herself.[34]

What is striking is that Etty seems to have had to overcome no fear in relation to God in order to find her center of stillness. This differentiates her from all the wounded women we discussed in the previous chapter. When the inner child is wounded, i.e., when a person lacks that fundamental expectation of goodness to which Simone Weil refers, she projects terrible images of God onto the void. In this case, as we saw, the person has to be distracted from those images and diverted from her fear, whether through the practice of art or some other spirit-engaging activity, in order to face the void. The turning point, for such a person, comes when she cries out the pain of her abandonment in the direction of the God that she fears. But Etty was not the least bit victimized by images of a dark God. The breakthrough for her was the discovery that human beings can be intimate with God, that there is a standpoint beyond that of self-consciousness where I am present to God and God is present to me. This passage was written just three days before Etty's "prayer of willingness": "The girl who could not kneel but learned to do so on the rough coconut matting in an untidy bathroom. Such things are often more intimate even than sex. The story of the girl who gradually learned to kneel is something that I would love to write in the fullest possible way."[35]

SAYING YES TO THE DESIRE OF THE HEART

When you are in the presence of God, you can think that you know the desire of your heart. To be with God, to commune with God, to feel that you are held in God's loving gaze—what more could a person want? It can seem that you are ready to die in moments of presence because you know that no earthly thing can give you as much. But here is the danger of an encounter with God that we alluded to at the beginning of the chapter. What is to prevent the desire for God from becoming a kind of death wish? Some of the mystics in the Christian tradition seem to have lived most of their lives with what Camus calls a "nostalgia for the eternal"[36] that gave them an other-worldly orientation. I think of Simone Weil, the contemporary mystic, who grew more and more removed from the things of life after her mystical experiences and finally starved herself to death. In her Gnostic vision of reality, the life-force, which draws us into this-worldly engagements, appears as a necessary evil. A passage in one of her notebooks contains the lament that life in the world—as opposed to life in solitude—cannot be as "pure, beautiful, and complete as a Greek statue."[37]

The person who keeps withdrawing from the world to be with God is like the lover who never wants to take her eyes from her beloved's face. The death wish enters in when one's desire for God masks a hatred or fear of life in the world—of the confinement, earthiness, and inevitable pain of human relationships. Ultimately, the person who flees into solitude is fleeing herself—the part of herself that is responsive to the life-force and desirous of relationships. Etty was one friend of God who never lost her equilibrium as a human being. As much as she seems to have sought out times for prayer, she never denied her need for human intimacy. This seems to be the recipe for discerning the true desire of your heart: being open to the presence of God while staying in touch with your human needs. When it is the whole heart that is consulted this way, what we realize is that we do not want God, exactly, but to walk with God. We are like the lover who does not want to lose herself in her beloved's gaze, but wants to be herself at her beloved's side.

In her "prayer of willingness," Etty is saying yes to her desire to walk with God. It was recorded the morning after she found herself "babbling it out" as she rode her bicycle through Amsterdam in the cold and dark:

God, take me by Your hand, I shall follow You duti-
fully, and not resist too much. I shall evade none of the
tempests life has in store for me, I shall try to face it all as
best I can. But now and then grant me a short respite. I
shall never again assume, in my innocence, that any peace
that comes my way will be eternal. I shall accept all the inevitable tumult and struggle. I delight in warmth and security, but I shall not rebel if I have to suffer cold, should You
so decree. I shall follow wherever Your hand leads me and
shall try not to be afraid. I shall try to spread some of my
warmth, of my genuine love for others, wherever I go. But
we shouldn't boast of our love for others. We cannot be
sure that it really exists. I don't want to be anything special,
I only want to try to be true to that in me which seeks to
fulfil its promise.[38]

What is refreshing about Etty's prayer is that it is not at all
self-effacing. She does not apologize to God for her needs,
much less attempt to deny them. Besides expressing trust in
God, it reflects confidence in her own innate goodness: something in her—which doesn't make her "special" and therefore
must be in everyone—is "seek[ing] to fulfil its promise."

The discovery of our own path, the sense of setting out
on a journey with God, centers us in such a way that we are
no longer dependent on others for spiritual direction. Spier
had always pointed Etty to her own soul and now, in the aftermath of her "prayer of willingness," she reports a sense of "complete emancipation from him, of continuing all by [her]self."[39]
Outwardly, their relationship did not change. She had gradually assumed the role of his secretary and in that capacity, had
had almost daily contact with him. Their work together would
continue until she left for Westerbork camp eight months
later. Inwardly, she no longer felt bound to him as her mentor.
It is fitting that Etty refers to her new freedom from Spier as
"emancipation." Until you have discovered the Living God
by withdrawing into your center of stillness, you have a slave's

mentality vis-à-vis the person to whom you have devoted yourself: instead of expressing yourself freely and spontaneously, you are constantly inhibited by your desire for the other's approval. Now, Etty says, she "listens in to [her]self, allows [her]self to be led, not by anything on the outside, but by what wells up from within."[40]

II. Integrating the Life-force by Participation in the Divine Life

Choosing the Personal over the Impersonal

Were a woman to discover her center of stillness without embracing the journey with God, instead of feeling that she was being led by God through life, it would seem that she simply had a special knowledge of God. Her discovery would reflect itself mainly in her increased sense of her own—and others'—inherent dignity and worth. "I found God in myself and I loved her fiercely."[41] This famous line from Ntozake Shange's book, *For Colored Girls Who Get Homesick Even When the Rainbow Is Enuf*, illustrates the kind of appropriation of the experience of God that many women are making today. Often coming from a background of oppression, whether as women or as persons of color or both, authors like Shange use the experience as a basis for empowerment, as a way of overcoming the self-hatred and despair that oppression spawns. Foremost among this group is Alice Walker, who describes her work as contributing to the "de-colonization of the human spirit."[42] Her portrait of Celie in *The Color Purple* is poignant in its evocation of the emergence of self-love in a woman whose spirit had been crushed by abusive men and authoritarian images of God.

Shange and Walker, it seems to me, are living out of the knowledge of their essential connection to God. In her advocacy for victims of oppression, Walker speaks with the conviction of someone who knows from her own experience that cruelty toward others is ontologically inappropriate. But it is one thing to live out of the knowledge of your essential connection to God and another to live out of the connection itself. Embracing the journey with God represents the latter choice. It turns the "connection" into a real relationship. In Etty's diary entries that represent a kind of summing up of the first stage of her spiritual journey, we find what seem to be references to the importance of making this choice. No less than three times she tells herself, in effect, that the change that has taken place in her is not enough, that she must also have "the courage to speak God's name."[43] It was Spier who first admonished her this way and his words keep coming back to her: "Now my inner world is all peace and quiet. It was a difficult road, though it all seems so simple and obvious now. One phrase has been haunting me for weeks: 'You must also have the courage to say openly that you believe; to say God.'"[44]

Why does it take courage to "speak God's name"? Spier told Etty that it had taken a long time before he had dared to say "God" without feeling that there was something ridiculous about it. Calling God by name means opening the heart to ultimate reality; it means relating to ultimate reality as Person. This seems ludicrous to modern individuals raised on the scientific conception of the universe, according to which reality is governed solely by impersonal forces. On this account, the rational or at least quasi-rational thing to do, when you have a religious experience, is to describe it in terms of supernatural forces. Spier himself did this once, according to Etty, in response to a young man who said that he sometimes felt that God was right inside him, such as when he would listen to the St. Matthew Passion. Spier said, "At such times you are completely at one with the creative and cosmic forces that are at work in every human being." But he went on to say that these creative forces were ultimately part of God.[45] Etty, too, in words that echo almost exactly Simone Weil's description of her first encounter with God[46] speaks in impersonal terms of a powerful prayer experience: "Last night, shortly before going to bed, I suddenly went down on my knees in the middle of this large room. . . . Almost automatically. Forced to the ground by something stronger than myself."[47]

Referring to experiences of God in terms of impersonal forces, besides making them less "ridiculous" according to modern ways of thinking, also allows you to distance yourself from their claim on your heart. In Simone Weil's spiritual evolution, it was not until one and a half years after her initial experience of God that she was able to say God's name.[48] One of her journal entries reveals the fear that inhibited her: "I need God to take me by force, because if death, doing away with the shield of the flesh, were to put me face to face with him, I should run away."[49] Some people dread a relationship with God, it seems to me, because it means living beyond the limits of what we can know. We have a need to know that God exists, to know that being transcends the limits of what we can know; the fulfillment of this need is the great value of religious experiences in which we get a glimpse—fleeting but real—of the mystery that surrounds our life and death. But to live in relation to that mystery, to give up the sense of control that goes with knowing—or thinking you know—what to expect from life, this is a choice that, to use the poet Susan Griffin's phrase from quite a different context, "cracks open the heart."[50] In an entry from December 1941 Etty seems to be sensing the radical disjuncture that her choice for the journey with God is making in her life: "I have truly reached my limits, I can go no further than I have already gone, the frontiers are too close and to cross them means heading straight for a mental institution. Or for death? But I haven't yet thought that far."[51]

Etty's words suggest that the choice for the journey with God, like every lover's choice, carries the presentiment of death. In the Eros and Psyche story, this is the meaning of the oracle's pronouncement that Psyche's bridegroom is to be a great beast. We tremble on the verge of giving our hearts to the unknown because this relinquishing anticipates the relinquishing of death. If, like Etty, we make the lover's choice, it is because we realize that the heart knows something that we don't know. "Within limits we can know," Wendell Berry writes. "Within somewhat wider limits we can imagine. We can extend compassion to the limit of imagination. We can love, it seems, beyond imagining."[52] What enables us to say yes to the journey with God, finally, is the love that soars beyond our imagining. For is not this love a kind of knowing? Does it not imply a larger life beyond the limits set by our minds? When we are led by the heart, we seem called to participate in that larger life. Shortly after Etty's "prayer of willingness," the first prayer recorded in her diary, we find this entry: "No longer: I want this or that, but: life is great and good and fascinating and eternal and if you dwell so much on yourself and flounder and fluff about, you miss the mighty, eternal current that is life."[53]

A woman blossoms when she gives her heart to the journey with God whether she does it in full consciousness like Etty or barely intuiting it—for example, as the deeper surrender implied by her yes to her husband. This is the point at which every woman is Psyche, a soul in love with a heavenly bridegroom. It is interesting that while Psyche's story begins with her ravishment by Eros, Etty's has a preliminary chapter. If Psyche is simply waiting on her soul before her meeting with Eros, Etty has to find her soul—she has to differentiate, as we have seen, between her desire for an "illusory absolute" and the true desire of her heart. Willingness to know one's heart is assumed in the ancient story, whereas Etty must fight through a current of unwillingness. In the afterglow of saying yes to the journey with God, "the girl who could not kneel" seems as contented as Psyche in her castle. "Oh God, I thank you for having created me as I am," she writes. "I thank you for the sense of fulfillment I sometimes have; that fulfillment is after all nothing but being filled with you."[54]

THE REDEMPTIVE POWER OF SUFFERING

To a person whose life has been determined by the un-harnessed power of the life-force—her spirit exultant and commanding when it waxed and diffuse when it waned—the choice for the journey with God provides, for the first time, a sense of direction. However marvelous her love affairs and ec-static experiences from the past, their gleam in her memory fades in comparison with the solemn feeling she has that the life she is meant to live is unfolding. "So, everything is no longer pure chance," Etty writes, "a bit of a game now and then, an exciting adventure. Instead, I have the feeling that I have a destiny, in which the events are strung significantly to-gether."[55] It is the vision of the larger life that gives you a sense of direction. The significance of events in your life de-rives from their resonance with this vision of the heart. Etty writes the above passage about her feeling of having a destiny as part of an extended reflection on an unexpected meeting she had with Max, the man with whom she had had an affair ten years earlier that ended with her "desperate."[56] She is gratified to find that from her new standpoint she no longer mourns her past love but is reconciled to it and can once again enjoy the man's presence. She describes the evening with him as "their first real meeting"[57] and says that now this person is not lost to her but can be part of her life.

Until I free the other person of my need for him, I am re-lating to him as he exists for me and not as he exists for him-self. This is the essence of an oppressive relation. But at the same time that I am objectifying the other I am imprisoning myself behind a wall of projections; I may think that I am knowing and loving the other but it is an image from my own fantasies to which I am relating. The journey with God repre-sents a higher standpoint than a way of life determined by one's needs. The heart's vision of a larger life frees me from the trammeling influence of my fantasies. But this allows me to truly encounter the other, and in that meeting a deep chord in my heart is struck. The image of the other as infinitely precious replaces the infernal image I have been carrying and this new image has a permanent place in my heart. As long as I stay in touch with my heart, I can find the other, or rather my love for the other, there. When Etty describes her encounter with her former lover as their "first real meeting," what is suggested is that the meaning of all our relationships is the love we experience in the pure encounter. My desperate attachment to the other is meant to become this love.

If it is the vision of a larger life that gives us the sense of a destiny, moments of pure love such as we are describing seem to confirm it. There is a hint of eternity in every genuine encounter. The resonance I feel in the presence of the other goes as deep as my God relation, and in our exchange I get a glimpse of our ultimate connectedness. Etty reflects that when she and Max were having an affair, she had been trying to cling "to something one cannot cling to with the body."[58] From our very first meeting, the presence of the other can strike a chord in me, but it is only when I am aware of the presence of God in myself that I can relate to the other with wonder and love instead of possessively. Etty found that all her friendships took on a deeper meaning after she embraced the journey with God. In one diary entry, thinking back over a party held the previous evening in honor of her brother, who was an accomplished pianist, she remembers having

> that strange feeling again: There sits Adri, I thought, and Tide over there, and there the Levies and S[pier], and Leonie on my left, and my little brother behind the piano, all my good friends around me and I felt a great bond with each one in a different way, a bond that was not a chain. And as a result so many inner forces were freed. So much inner freedom and independence, and finding myself so immersed and happy and strong.[59]

But here is the difficulty. Just like Psyche, who fell more passionately in love with Eros when she recognized his divine nature, we may find that our desire for the other increases once we recognize the presence of God in him. It is a pure desire in that we are no longer dominated by the need to possess the other, but it is passionate. We simply want to be with the other. We want to feel the heart's resonance continually. The ideal life, it seems, would be the journey with God with the other as a companion. One of the reasons that Etty was able to relate to her former lover Max with such equanimity is that her passion had found a new focus in her friendship with Spier. Having broken away from Spier as a mentor by establishing her own relationship with God, Etty found herself more drawn to him than ever but in a different way: "A gradual change from the physical to the spiritual," she writes in an entry from March 1942.[60] And "the sexual and erotic element in me has gradually been conditioned to play a subordinate role to human warmth, although that warmth is intense and passionate enough."[61]

The difficulty in a relationship such as Etty came to have with Spier is that in order to keep your passion pure, you must have the strength to continually let go of the other. This is the discipline of all true love. While the need to possess the other is no longer dominant once one has established a relationship with God, it is still there, for the heart craves presence—the other's image is not enough. So we suffer absences, separations, the other's unavailability. Etty never lost sight of the fact that for all their daily contact and increasing closeness, she and Spier did not have a future together. He was firmly committed to his fiancée in England. An entry from April 1942 reveals how painful this situation could be for her:

> Last night before falling asleep I asked myself if I did not live too reckless a life. In London there is a girl he intends to make his wife. Inwardly, I live in complete independence and freedom from him and I tell myself that I can go my own way in the world, but will I really be able to go

on living away from the warmth of the rays that emanate
from the very centre of his being? When I thought about it
very hard last night, in bed, shortly before falling asleep, I
felt that I would not, and then my face was suddenly wet
with tears and there was a longing in me that was as heavy
as lead.[62]

Some of us instinctively guard our hearts when we anticipate the loss of the one we love. But Etty kept hers open
to Spier. A true Psyche, she seems to have known that suffering and love go together. At a time when many people were
probably withdrawing from relationships, giving in to the
sense of futility you have when circumstances are beyond your
control, Etty seems to have entered more fully into all her
relationships—"the friends, my many friends," she writes.
"Nowadays there are hardly any accidental relationships left;
you have a deep if subtly different relationship with each person, and must not be disloyal to one for the sake of the other.
There are no wasted and boring minutes any longer."[63] Continuing to love, Etty realized, is the most beautiful act of rebellion one can perform in an oppressive situation. The oppressor
wants to maim and crush your spirit and insofar as you succumb to hatred and despair, he has succeeded. She saw so
clearly that hatred and despair are ways that we keep ourselves
from having to suffer. She imagines herself saying to a friend of
hers who has lost a son in a concentration camp, "you must be
able to bear your sorrow; even if it seems to crush you, you will
be able to stand up again for human beings are so strong, and
your sorrow must become an integral part of yourself."[64]

It can seem strange to think that there might be a gain
in bearing your sorrow, in embracing the pain of loss and separation. Some sorrows strike us as overwhelming—we think of
Psyche being tempted repeatedly to end her life after her separation from Eros. To suffer without doing harm to your spirit,
you have to have "a mind for suffering" according to Samuel
Lamb, a Christian pastor in China who was imprisoned for

twenty-one years because of his faith. "If you have a mind to suffer, you can stand it," he says, "but if you don't . . . you can be broken."[65] It is the vision of a larger life that creates a "mind for suffering," it seems. Unlike the dream of "happily ever after"—the projection of our fantasies into the future which excludes suffering—the heart's vision of the larger life comprehends suffering. Living by the dream, suffering is felt simply as a diminishment and so, like Sylvia Plath, we instinctively rebel against it. But her spirit was ultimately broken, we saw, by the losses she experienced. Living out of the vision, suffering increases our reliance on our essential self or God-relation and the more we rely on it, the more the power of our God-relation is felt in our lives.

Etty's reliance on her essential self or God-relation was clearly what kept her from letting the dark power of the hag-queen—our instinctual rage against suffering and death—take over in her life. In a very early diary entry, she confesses that hatred of the Germans sometimes caused her to act cruelly towards her housemate Kathe, who was German. She would find herself "cursing and swearing," she says, when reading the newspapers or hearing the reports of what was happening and would realize that she was doing it deliberately to "work off her anger" by hurting Kathe.[66] At this point she recognizes the self-destructiveness of abandoning herself to her anger: "Indiscriminate hatred is the worst thing there is," she writes. "It is a sickness of the soul."[67] But it is only after her discovery of the presence of God at the center of herself and her yes to the journey with God that she is able to find an antidote to the power of her anger. In the conversation she imagines herself having with the friend who has lost a son, she seems to imply that there is a way to suffer by which we not only contain our instinctual rage, but also transcend it:

> Give your sorrow all the space and shelter in yourself that is its due, for if everyone bears his grief honestly and courageously, the sorrow that now fills the world will abate. But

if you do not clear a decent shelter for your sorrow, and instead reserve most of the space inside you for hatred and thoughts of revenge—from which new sorrows will be born for others—then sorrow will never cease in this world and will multiply. And if you have given sorrow the space its gentle origins demand, then you may truly say: life is beautiful and so rich. So beautiful and so rich that it makes you want to believe in God.[68]

The last two sentences in the above passage hint at a deeper life to which we have access by opening our hearts to suffering. Until I suffer, my love of God does not penetrate the dark side of my heart, the region of the instincts where I crave life and fear death, where the power of the life-force seems irresistible. Instead, it coexists with my dependency on the life-force so that there seem to be two different currents or sources of energy running through my life. Meinrad Craighead, the artist and former Benedictine nun, seems to be referring to this kind of duality in the distinction she makes between "Mothergod" and "Fathergod." "Mothergod" she identifies as "that force living within me which is more real, more powerful than the remote Fathergod," who is associated with her "Catholic heritage and environment which have been like a beautiful river flowing over my subterranean foundation in God the Mother."[69] What Craighead is bringing out here is that our reliance on the life-force is more natural to us than our reliance on our God-relation and the love that flows from that. The life-force is elemental. When Craighead lights a fire in the vessel in the shape of a woman's body that sits upon her outdoor altar and offers her prayers for the day, she seems to be participating in that "deep magic from the dawn of time" to which C. S. Lewis refers.

My love of God and my instinctual reliance on the life-force may not be experienced as opposing tendencies for a long time. Craighead, for example, in her introduction to *The Mother's Songs*, her extremely sensual collection of drawings celebrating the female body, writes about her experiences of

"Mothergod" and "Fathergod," "The two movements are not in conflict, they simply water different layers in my soul."[70] They can come into conflict, however, through the experience of suffering. When I suffer, I instinctively shield myself from the diminishment of suffering by wielding the life-force in the form of rage. But rage, of course, is incompatible with the pure love the idea of God evokes in me once I have encountered the Living God at my center of stillness. Thus suffering reveals the disunity of my being: I am the woman who loves God, on the one hand, and I am the woman filled with hatred on account of my situation, on the other. How can I become the whole woman, I ask myself, whose love of God allows her to be at peace even in an impossible situation? Like Psyche, Etty seems to have always known that the only solution to the problem of suffering is to suffer—to suffer willingly, that is, trusting that my love of God will sustain me even in the region of the instincts. This is such a simple solution, yet there is a tendency in all of us to resist it and the heart of the matter is the issue of power. All human beings, Simone Weil says, have a natural tendency to do whatever is necessary to preserve or increase our feeling of power.[71] Opening our hearts to suffering means going against this natural tendency. It means accepting a situation of powerlessness. To the extent that we identify with our feeling of power, the acceptance of powerlessness is virtually impossible. I will wield dark power before I will allow myself to experience diminishment. Even when my love of God provides a different basis for my identity, I can still rebel in a situation of suffering. I can refuse to follow a path that requires me to identify, as well, with my capacity for diminishment.

When we embrace suffering, we widen the circle of self-relation; love of God meets the resistance to love and gradually de-fangs it. Then we carry our resistance to love as a way of being more deeply in touch with others. We resonate with their wretchedness as well as with their beauty. Underneath the cruelty others may enact, we intuit their wretchedness.

Herein is what we could call the redemptive power of suffering: once I embrace the dark side of myself, darkness in the other is no longer a barrier to relationship. Over and over Etty stresses that the failure of people to allow themselves to be deepened by suffering is contributing to the evil of the war:

> All disasters stem from us. Why is there a war? Perhaps because now and then I might be inclined to snap at my neighbour. Because I and my neighbour and everyone else do not have enough love. Yet we could fight war and all its excrescences by releasing, each day, the love that is shackled inside us, and giving it a chance to live. And I believe I will never be able to hate any human being for his so-called "wickedness," that I shall only hate the evil that is within me, though hate is perhaps putting it too strongly even then.[72]

Moral indignation is different from hatred, Etty points out, but one must examine one's motives to make sure that the former is not just a mask for the latter.

When we claim our dark side, we have such a sense of having joined the human circle, of being able to relate to all kinds of people, because we ourselves are in touch with what every human being is: light and darkness; love and resistance to love. Being-in-touch is its own kind of power. Instead of enthralling people, it calls forth from them their own wholeness, their own embrace of the bad as well as the good in themselves. This is the power that Etty saw in Spier as he worked with his patients: "He breaks them open and draws out the poison and delves down to the sources where God hides himself away. And he works with such intensity that, in the end, the water of life begins to flow again in dried-up souls; each day the life-stories pile up on his little table, almost every one ending with Please help me."[73] When we let our love of God encompass our resistance to love, it is indeed an experience of new life flowing within us: however obdurate the resistance, it is undercut by a deeper channel of love.

By suffering willingly, we tap into that "deeper magic from before the dawn of time" of which C. S. Lewis writes.[74] To open ourselves to suffering, we have to believe that the pure love of God in our hearts will not be extinguished by our hatred and our fear. We have to believe that the love will sustain us in the midst of the darkness of suffering. It is precisely by believing in it, by relying on it, that we discover the true nature of our love of God. When Etty speaks in wonderment of "that radiant feeling inside [her], which encompasses but is untouched by all the suffering and all the violence,"[75] she seems to have made that discovery. That pure love which arises out of the encounter between me and the presence of God at the center of myself, out of my yes to that encounter, is mine by participation. My yes opens a channel to the love in my life; the love itself is already there. I only realize this fully when I open myself to the dark side of life, for then what I experience is the love sustaining me. My yes in the midst of the darkness of suffering allows the love to encompass my whole self. It is by being encompassed, I realize, that I continue to stand in the midst of suffering, I do not stand on my own.

Once I know that my love of God can encompass my resistance to love, it seems to me that as long as I rely on that love, I am unassailable. Etty's diary entries on the subject of how a person can retain her inner freedom despite oppressive circumstances are emphatic. Referring to her situation of persecution as a Jew, she writes:

> They can harrass us, they can rob us of our material goods, of our freedom of movement, but we ourselves forfeit our greatest assets by our misguided compliance. By our feelings of being persecuted, humiliated, and oppressed. By our own hatred. By our swagger, which hides our fear. We may of course be sad and depressed by what has been done to us; that is only human and understandable. However: our greatest injury is one we inflict upon ourselves. I find life beautiful and I feel free. The sky within me is as wide as the one stretching above my head.[76]

In another passage, she seems to be linking her self-assurance more explicitly to the emergence of a deeper life within herself:

> I sometimes bow my head under the great burden that weighs down on me, but even as I bow my head I also feel the need, almost mechanically, to fold my hands. And so I can sit for hours and know everything and bear everything and grow stronger in the bearing of it, and at the same time feel sure that life is beautiful and worth living and meaningful. Despite everything. But that does not mean I am always filled with joy and exaltation. I am often dog-tired after standing in queues, but I know that this too is part of life and *somewhere there is something inside me that will never desert me again.* (original italics)[77]

THE DEEPER LIFE OF SPIRIT

My experience of a love that encompasses and sustains me in the midst of the darkness of suffering is an experience of spirit, of the deeper life of spirit. It is through spirit that I participate in "the deeper magic from before the dawn of time." When I am relying on spirit and look inward, I feel the encompassing and sustaining love as my true foundation. When I am relying on spirit and look outside myself, I feel the love as my connection to all things. Along with her friendships, Etty cherished what she describes in one place as her "intimate relationship" with the tree outside her bedroom window. She admits that she can't talk about it to "every Tom, Dick and Harry,"[78] but its importance to her is clear. "Sometimes my day is crammed full of people and talk and yet I have the feeling of living in utter peace and quiet. And the tree outside my window, in the evenings, is a greater experience than all those people put together."[79] We can imagine that this "greater experience" to which Etty refers begins with the stab at the heart that we all feel in the presence of beauty. But then it opens out into one of those moments when the separation between human beings and nature is overcome, when instead of simply looking at the world as at a beautiful picture, I know myself as part of the world, I am in the picture.

When Etty is feeling her connection to nature, she refers to the current of love within her in feminine terms: "I went to bed early last night and from my bed I stared out through the large open window. And it was once more as if life with all its mysteries was close to me, as if I could touch it. I had the feeling that I was resting against the naked breast of life, and could feel her gentle and regular heartbeat. I felt safe and protected."[80] This passage is reminiscent of Meinrad Craighead's references to "Mothergod," which we interpreted, however, not in terms of the deeper life of spirit but in terms of the life-force. Craighead and Etty may be referring to the same thing. I believe, however, that Craighead's experience of "Mothergod" is simply a pure experience of the life-force. By that I mean that it is possible to feel the tremendous power of one's desire for life and to become centered on the desire itself instead of on any object of one's desire. This is a fascinating experience. Feminist Audre Lorde recommends it as a way for women to free themselves from the repressive institutions of a "patriarchal and anti-erotic society."[81]

It is important to distinguish between Etty's experiences of the deeper life of the spirit and the pure experience of the life-force because a woman seeking her true self might be misled by the fascination of the latter. Let us imagine a woman quite different from Etty, whose sexuality has been repressed because of her fear of men. Her first experience of the free unfolding of desire within herself will seem holy simply because she has never felt alive in this region of her instincts. It may seem to her that to fail to pursue this desire would be to dishonor herself by settling for something less than a vital existence. This is exactly how Audre Lorde views the matter: The erotic "is an internal sense of satisfaction to which, once we have experienced it, we know we can aspire. For having experienced the fullness of this depth of feeling and recognizing its power, in honor and self-respect we can require no less of ourselves."[82] The authentic life for women, according to Lorde, involves refusing to exercise our power of eros in the service of men and using it to create a richly satisfying existence for ourselves.

Someone fascinated by the life-force might interpret Etty's experiences of oneness with nature as a transference of her power of eros from the sexual realm to the aesthetic realm. To be sure, Etty was uninhibited enough that she describes herself, in a passage in which she confesses to strong feelings of attraction for a young woman, as "erotic in all directions."[83] And certainly, the beauty of nature can provoke the slow uncurling of erotic desire in me so that the tree and I, the cat and I seem to be charged with the same energy. There is no doubt that Etty's experiences of connection with nature encompassed the body. But were they primarily erotic? I think not. When you are relying on spirit, the deeper life of spirit, the perception of beauty brings you to an experience of heart's ease. The sensation of desire gives way to a feeling of wholeness. It is like drinking tea with an old friend or feeling the sweet weight of a baby in your arms. We know, in moments of heart's ease, that life is good; it is not just, it is certainly not fair, but it is good. And this is a knowledge in which our bodies participate. In moments of heart's ease, mind and body are one in me through the deeper life.

A celebration of the deeper life appears again and again in Etty's diary after her discovery of the value of suffering. A spirit of gentleness pervades these passages which contrast with what she calls the "childish romanticism" of some of the others. Etty is still susceptible to flights of fantasy: she imagines binding herself to Spier in a "pretend marriage" and then "surrendering him unharmed" to his fiancée after the war and traveling the world alone.[84] But frequently, the voice of the mature woman is heard, speaking out of the deeper life: "Through suffering I have learned that we must share our love with the whole of creation. Only thus do we gain admittance to it."[85] The encompassing and sustaining love which I experience when I open my heart to suffering, when I let go of the pristine self-image that suffering and diminishment belie, is mine to enjoy only as long as I stay open. And that means relating to everyone out of the encompassing and sustaining love, refusing to get caught in the contraction of desire. Etty was sometimes flooded with the feeling of a love that makes us accessible to others and others accessible to us. Trying to identify her state of mind during an evening in the company of some new acquaintances, she rules out eroticism and the piquing of her vanity and finally realizes that what she felt was

> exaltation that all kinds of human beings should feel free to open themselves to me, that no human being is alien to me any longer, that I can find my way to people of every sort. And that, after all, isn't vanity but joyful love for all the many kinds of people and happiness because I shall always be able to find my way to each one of them.[86]

If a pristine self-conception limits the scope of your concern to your own time and place, to the course of your own lifetime, letting go of your ego-ideal allows your compassion to extend to the stranger, to the person you will never meet. Just as her connection to the natural world and to her friends gave her joy, Etty's feeling of connection to the people being persecuted while she was safe at her desk was painful: "Tonight . . . I lay in the dark with burning eyes as scene after scene of human suffering passed before me."[87] In her reflections on her experiences of entering into the suffering of others—really, going back and forth between suffering and joy—she seems to be saying that it is the connection that is important, not whether it brings one pain or joy. More and more, she was living deep down in her heart, we can see, where she knew herself not through the things of her life, but through the love that sustained her through all things. From this perspective,

what happens to us, even death, seems relatively and not absolutely important:

> when we are deprived of our lives, are we really deprived of
> very much? We have to accept death as part of life, even
> the most horrible of deaths. And don't we live an entire life
> each one of our days, and does it really matter if we live a
> few days more or less? I am in Poland every day. . . . I often
> see visions of poisonous green smoke; I am with the hungry,
> with the ill-treated and the dying, every day, but I am also
> with the jasmine and with that piece of sky beyond my
> window.[88]

The freedom that goes with my differentiation from the
things of my life is immense: I can let go of my life! All my
life, it seems to me, I have been living under the burden of
having to hold on to this life. Now that I realize that I am
spirit, it seems to me that I am held: the encompassing and
sustaining love promises to preserve me even when my life in
time is over. The relative value of the things of my life does
not mean that they are unimportant; on the contrary, to be
in this time and place, on this stretch of the human journey
seems utterly important as the means for me to express the
encompassing and sustaining love. The love is there in our
hearts—God is in our hearts, Etty would say—but it is we
who must give the love expression. The meaning of my life in
time, I see, is to express the love whose origin is beyond time.
Everywhere around her, Etty must have been hearing people
question God or even curse God for the suffering they were
having to endure. Because of her experience of the deeper
life, she could say, as she does in a diary entry from late June
1942, "God is not accountable to us for the senseless harm we
cause one another. We are accountable to Him."[89]

The question of how to express the love she felt in her
heart came to the forefront for Etty after she awakened to the
reality of spirit. For months she had been assisting Spier in his
work with his patients as well as supporting herself by teaching

Russian grammar. We can imagine that Etty could have continued these occupations even after her discovery of spirit. Instead of performing them out of the necessity of her desire to be with Spier, on the one hand, and her need to make a living, on the other, now she could have given herself freely to Spier's work of healing and to her students. But when we awaken to our essential self, to spirit, we awaken also to our essential desire. We feel heart's desire from the depths of the heart, where it is felt as what John Dunne calls a "deep loneliness."[90] How can I experience the encompassing and sustaining love and be lonely? Because all of me does not participate in the love. In the region of the instincts, I am still closed to the love, I am still dark. The deep loneliness is my heart's desire felt in the region of the instincts. From its first appearance in her life, Etty seems to have recognized that it was the deep loneliness that held the clue to the next stage of her journey. Here is her first reference to it:

> Life may be brimming over with experiences, but somewhere, deep inside, all of us carry a vast and fruitful loneliness wherever we go. And sometimes the most important thing in a whole day is the rest we take between two deep breaths, or the turning inwards in prayer for five short minutes.[91]

In calling this deep loneliness "fruitful," Etty seems to recognize it as a desire for God, to be caught up in God, to participate more fully in the encompassing and sustaining love. As loneliness, John Dunne points out, the desire is ineffectual; it only makes me realize how incomplete, how lacking in passion my love of God is. Unrecognized, the deep loneliness can simply make me feel that I am never satisfied, that I am doomed to a restless search for something I can never find, but when I recognize it, as Etty seems to have done, it can provoke a crisis in my life. I am open to God, I realize, I have said yes to the journey with God, but my yes is only partial; it does not comprehend the deep loneliness. I am afraid to let my desire for God become effectual, become a "powerful longing," as John Dunne puts it, for it will then become the ruling passion of my life. Do I want the love of God to be my ruling passion? "Love is total, my friend, carrying us forever where it goes," the Sufi mystic Al-Hallaj says in the play by Herbert Mason. "It is not experimental and it knows no term."[92] A woman's trembling in giving her heart to the journey with God indicates her awareness of death on the path she is choosing. Opening her heart to encompass the deep loneliness represents her integration of death on her path.

BEING HEART AND SOUL ON THE JOURNEY WITH GOD

Because of her reliance on the deeper life of spirit, Etty does not seem to have felt fear so much in connection with saying yes to the deep loneliness as sadness over the separation from her beloved Spier that saying yes to it would entail. For a period of several months, she seems to have been alternately drawn to him—as the most beautiful being she knew—and pushed away from him by the intensity of the loneliness she felt when they were together. A diary entry from April 1942 reveals that she sometimes "kept him at arm's length," because of her usual inability to express physically the depth of feeling he awakened in her and that she was "always so sad" after they had physical contact. The same entry concludes with this account of how the previous evening, which she had spent mainly with Spier, had ended:

> Last night when I cycled home from S., I poured out all my tenderness, all the tenderness one cannot express for a man even when one loves him very, very much, I poured it all out into the great all-embracing spring night. I stood on the little bridge and looked across the water; I melted into the landscape and offered all my tenderness up to the sky and the stars and the water and to the little bridge. And that was the best moment of the day.[93]

The image of a woman freely offering all her tenderness up to the night sky—how similar and yet dissimilar this is to the image of the adulterous wife from Camus's story with which we began this chapter. Both women are enacting a desire for God, but the woman in Camus's story does not really know God. Bursting forth from the desperation she feels over her life in the human circle, she is blind in her desire while Etty is knowing. The difference between the two standpoints is the journey with God. After her initial encounter with God—as the holy mystery at the center of herself—Etty let the love that arose from that encounter transform her relationships: she began to relate to others out of her heart's desire for God instead of her needs. She began to rely on heart's desire rather than the life-force. When you do this, you discover traces of God—signs of the mysterious life—in everyone. But God in the other comes and goes, appears and disappears. Ultimately, the beautiful person that you love, because he both is and is not God, makes you turn your gaze to the One who is. There is a journey ahead of the adulterous wife. It is the journey from God in herself to God in the other to the One beyond self and other in whom the other and self are. Without the journey, in which the life-force and heart's desire are differentiated, I do not come to know God as the One who is.

The differentiation of the life-force and heart's desire begins in me as soon as I start to rely on my heart's desire. Until then, my experience of God, whether through myself or through others, simply reinforces my attachment to life. In this case, when I speak of God, I mean the One who is the source of life. A woman giving birth, for example, can have a powerful experience of God as source of life. In her, heart's desire and the life-force undifferentiated produce ecstasy. In the imagery of the goddess tradition, it is an instance of the serpent itself praising God. When I associate God with life, I will throw myself, body and soul, into the service of life. Death will be my enemy. But when the life-force and heart's desire are differentiated, first by the journey inward where I know myself as known by God and then, through suffering, where I know myself as loved by God, I connect God with spirit, with my own capacity for knowing and loving. The love of God felt in my heart, i.e., my feeling of being encompassed and sustained, even in the midst of suffering, is a precious gift that I want to share with everyone. The love overflows in me when I am with others; it rises up in me when I am alone. The term of the encompassing and sustaining love, the term of heart's desire, I can see, is beyond the opposition of life and death; it is the larger life of spirit. Through my vision of the larger life, I know that I am and you are and God is.

What, then, of the problem of death? When I awaken to the larger life of spirit, how do I relate to the deep loneliness and death? I could, of course, deny its significance. I could identify the deep loneliness with life in the body and declare myself essentially free from it as spirit. This would be a Gnostic solution to the problem of the deep loneliness. Viewed this way, my deep loneliness and death would be an accidental rather than an integral aspect of my self-existence. The pain of my deep loneliness, the wrenching experience of death, would have no value for me; I would simply have to endure them as part and parcel of my life in the body. Although Etty sometimes sounds like a Gnostic in her new-found freedom of spirit, her conviction that she had to break with Spier—and embrace the deep loneliness—indicates that she was not. Despite her dreams of a "pretend marriage" to Spier that would enable them to be together throughout the war, she could be extremely lucid about the impediment her continuing attachment to him posed for her spiritual growth. As she saw it, it kept her from realizing her unique potential:

> Later on, he will have to thrust me away, push me towards my own inner space. In a flash of insight, it is suddenly clear to me: I must not long to spend my whole life with him, nor seek to marry him. It is thanks to him that I have found a way of expressing myself, but he must release me

again into a cosmic space where I can discover another expression, one that is purely my own.[94]

An "expression . . . purely [her] own" would be one that issued freely from her deepest desire, from the "vast and fruitful loneliness" that Etty was experiencing. In realizing that she would have to break with Spier, Etty was recognizing, it seems, the way that passion for another, or rather, attachment to the other who was the object of her passion, prevented her from saying yes to the deep loneliness. As long as I am clinging to the other, I am shielded from the deep loneliness and death. My attachment to the other keeps my love of God from going as deep as my deep loneliness—it keeps my love of God from becoming "fruitful." But how can I let go of the object of my passion? My attachment is instinctual; it indicates my continued reliance on the life-force. As much as I want my love of God to encompass the deep loneliness, I cannot help but fear it. I cannot imagine proceeding through life depending utterly on the love of God—with no residual reliance on the life-force. No wonder Etty could only envision her ultimate separation from Spier as a "release," as something that would be done to her. "Oh, to let someone you love go entirely free," she writes, "to leave him to live his own life, is the most difficult thing there is in this world."[95]

In the end, it was the reality of death, like a dark intruder into Etty's life, that effected her release from Spier. After months of dreaming of a future for herself beyond the war, Etty came to the realization, in July 1942, that death was her future. "Yes, I am still at the same desk," she writes, in a passage dated July 3rd, "but it seems to me that I am going to have to draw a line under everything and continue in a different tone. I must admit a new insight into my life and find a place for it, what is at stake is our impending destruction and annihilation, we can have no more illusions about that. They are out to destroy us completely."[96] Just as we instinctively grab hold of the beautiful person who stirs up the power of the life-force in us, so the entrance of the power of death into our lives causes an attenuation of that attachment. Death on the horizon is an ally of the life-force—it spurs me to create more and stronger attachments; but death right in front of me— when I am open to its reality—negates the life-force. It thus becomes an ally of my heart's desire for God.

There is a marvelous stillness felt when the reality of death is accepted. It is the stillness of someone who need not strive, who need not cling to anyone nor anything for protection. A yes to death releases your grip on all the people that you love so that instead of being "hard and tight-fisted and grasping," as D. H. Lawrence puts it, you have a "gentle reverence for the return gift."[97] A few days after Etty recorded her momentous insight of July 3rd, she felt the entrance of death into her relationship with Spier:

> He leant against the wall of Dicky's room and I leant gently and lightly against him, just as I had done on countless similar occasions in the past, but this time it suddenly felt as if the sky had fallen as in a Greek tragedy. For a moment my senses were totally confused and I felt as though I was standing with him in the centre of infinite space—pervaded by threats but also filled with eternity. In that moment, a great change took place within us, forever.[98]

Death accepted is like a hand gently laid on your heart that extinguishes all but your essential desire. It centers you in your heart's desire so that for the first time, it encompasses the deep loneliness. It comes home to you that the journey with God is a journey through death, that death is an integral part of the journey. "We have embraced a new reality," Etty writes, in the passage that describes the final change in her relationship with Spier. "All that matters now is to be kind to each other with all the goodness that is in us. And every encounter is also a farewell."[99]

When our love of God encompasses the deep loneliness, it seems as though a great energy has been harnessed for the journey with God. It is the energy of the serpent, the energy of the life-force. Our desire for life is not really negated when we say yes to death, rather, it is given a new orientation. It becomes the desire for God felt in the body. Now, as I travel my path, I am pierced anew by each beautiful person I meet, but the love I feel for them does not divide me because now my whole heart—even the part of my heart that feels with the body—knows that it wants God. The body knows God, can only know God, as life. When I say yes to my tremendous desire for life, I am seeking God through my body. I am seeking God, but I do not know God. It is only when I am differentiated from my body, when I awaken to myself as spirit, that I begin to know God. Through my spirit, I know God as love; indeed, it is my experience of the encompassing and sustaining love preserving me intact in the midst of suffering that enables me to differentiate myself from my body. Saying yes to the deep loneliness, saying yes to death represents the willingness that the love of God be manifest in my body. This willingness is transformative. It reveals the common root of my desire for life and my desire for God. The deep loneliness, we have said, is my essential desire. When I say yes to it, I know the love of God as life. What I was seeking blindly through my obedience to the life-force and what I began to know as I differentiated myself from the life-force, I know truly in the experience of a love that is life to my soul. The deep loneliness as love is life to my soul.

Shortly after her insight into the inevitable destruction of Dutch Jews, Etty accepted a position as typist on the Jewish Council of Amsterdam, an organization which mediated between the Nazis and the mass of Jews in Holland. The Council was responsible for determining which Jews should be sent to "labor camps" and which should be spared because deemed indispensable at home. She had applied for the position at the insistence of her brother, who clearly saw the job as a way for Etty's own life to be spared, but from the time that she submitted her application, she had misgivings:

My letter of application to the Jewish Council . . . has upset my cheerful yet deadly serious equilibrium. As if I had done something underhand. Like crowding on to a small piece of wood adrift on an endless ocean after a shipwreck and then saving oneself by pushing others into the water and watching them drown. It is all so ugly. And I don't think much of this particular crowd, either. I would much rather join those who prefer to float on their backs for awhile, drifting on the ocean with their eyes turned toward heaven and who then go down with a prayer.[100]

After only a few weeks in what she called "that madhouse"[101] Etty volunteered to accompany a group of Jews to Westerbork, a transport camp for people whose ultimate destination was Auschwitz. For awhile, she went back and forth between Amsterdam and Westerbork. On one of her visits home, she attended the death and funeral of Spier, who had grown suddenly ill while she was in Westerbork. Her last diary entries were written in the aftermath of Spier's death while she was still in Amsterdam, recuperating from an illness that had kept her from returning immediately to the transport camp.

In these entries, we see Etty gradually coming to an understanding of the change that has taken place within her. Reflecting on Spier's passing, she realizes that she is now standing in the place where he once stood for her: "You were the mediator between God and me and now you, the mediator, have gone and my path leads straight to God. It is right that it should be so. And I shall be the mediator for any other soul I can reach."[102] If Etty had not embraced the deep loneliness, she would still be clinging to Spier—to his image—after his death. And he would still be coming between her and God. She goes on to indicate in this entry that images of Spier actually make her uncomfortable: "A portrait of you hangs on my wall. I want to tear it up and throw it away. To be closer to you."[103] When the life of soul is new-born in a person, images of God or one's God-figure can be annoying. The response to their beauty, which set you on the path to God, seems shallow compared to the love you feel when the deep loneliness is enkindled. "I want to put all your portraits away," Etty continues, "and never look at them again, for they are so much dead matter. I want to carry you in me, nameless, and pass you on with a new and tender gesture I did not know before."[104]

Etty's words about carrying Spier within her nameless make sense only if the dead we love are somehow alive to us in the love that is life to our souls. We think of Archbishop Oscar Romero's statement, "If they kill me, I shall rise again in the Salvadoran people."[105] And of course, there is the retort of Jesus to the Saducees, "Have you never read what God himself said to you: 'I am the God of Abraham, the God of Isaac, and the God of Jacob?' God is God, not of the dead, but of the living."[106] When the deep loneliness becomes love in me, there is no separation between me and God; in the love, God and I are one. So it seems to me that I am one with everyone who loves God, who overcomes the fear of death and aloneness and says yes to her essential desire. As she was preparing herself to attend Spier's funeral, Etty realized that she was not sad. Her experience of the love that is life to our souls gave her a new sense of mission: "I shall live on with that part of the dead that lives forever, and I shall enkindle into life that of the living which is now dead, until there is nothing but life, one great life, oh God."[107]

Most of Etty's reflections, in these last diary entries, involve Westerbork, the transport camp where she had spent what she describes as "the two richest and most intense months of my life."[108] The deep loneliness enkindled is a powerful passion and being prevented from giving it expression is painful. Etty chafed at the delay of her return to Westerbork, at the same time marveling that a transport camp should have become the place she most desired to be:

> How is it that this stretch of heathland surrounded by barbed wire, through which so much human misery has flooded, nevertheless remains inscribed in my memory

as something almost lovely? How is it that my spirit, far from being oppressed, seemed to grow lighter and brighter there?[109]

Being Etty, she considers one more time the possibility of devoting herself and the love she feels to a man. But this time, the idea seems "childish." "Is it very arrogant of me," she asks, "to say that I have too much love in me to give it all to just one person?"[110] Here is the most significant divergence of Etty's story from Psyche's. Psyche, on her return from the underworld, opens the casket of beauty ointment from Persephone and falls into a state of unconsciousness, which allows Eros to rescue her. She has faced death, she has experienced the enkindling of a divine passion within herself, but half afraid, perhaps, of the power of her passion, she returns to the same place she left. She does not give her soul's passion free rein. Etty, by contrast, realizes that to return to the dream of devoting herself to a man would be to force her life into a configuration that she had outgrown. Was Etty inspired by the example of Jesus in her fearless choice of a path that would bring her certain death? We know that she was reading the Gospel of Matthew "morning and night"[111] and that when accused by one of her friends of expounding Christianity, she replied, "Yes, Christianity, and why ever not?"[112] Her decision for Westerbork seems all the more amazing when we realize that it involved the rejection of a path that might have meant freedom from the Nazis for her. In an entry from early October 1942, we find:

And now it seems that I have been 'exempted'. "Am I expected to jump for joy?" I asked the lawyer with the short leg. I don't want that scrap of paper for which most Jews would give their right arm, I don't want it in the least, so why should it have dropped into mine of all laps? I want to be sent to every one of the camps that lie scattered all over Europe, I want to be at every front, I don't ever want to be what they call 'safe'. . .

The entry concludes, "And I can, if You will only let me get healthy, oh Lord."[113] Whether she thought of herself as standing in the place of Jesus or not, Etty's desire to move out of the sanctuary of her desk and circle of friends in Amsterdam into the mass of suffering humanity at Westerbork is reminiscent of the desire to touch and heal people that we see impelling Jesus throughout his public ministry. Her diary ends with the sentence, "We should be willing to act as a balm for all wounds."[114]

When the desire for God, for the journey with God, has become a passion, there are moments when you have a taste of the "abundant life" that Jesus promised his followers.[115] What we have to understand about Etty or anyone who succeeds in saying yes to her essential desire is that what seem to be heroic choices are really choices for the abundant life. In explaining why he continued to practice civil disobedience, going to prison again and again for his opposition to nuclear weapons, Daniel Berrigan wrote, "for the sheer joy of it."[116] There is a joy that is deeper than the fulfillment of your dreams. If Sylvia Plath's journey shows that we can die from our dreams of love when they go unfulfilled, Etty's reveals that we can experience a love that is beyond our dreams. Nothing prepares us for that implosion of the heart followed by fire. Or are we prepared? There is discontinuity and continuity, I want to say, between Sylvia Plath's infernal dreams and Etty's taste of heaven. Both are forms of heart's desire, but with Plath, the heart does not know what it truly desires. The journey Etty traveled from falling in love with Spier to falling in love—if we may put it that way—with God, was simply the process of coming to know her heart. The shattering of our dreams does not break the heart if we are willing to embrace another, deeper life. On the eve of her return to Westerbork and certain death in a concentration camp, Etty was only grateful. "Sometimes it bursts into full flame within me," she writes.[117]

S I X

The Goddess Trajectory to Christianity

There is a beautiful story by Rilke which describes the recovery of God in our time. He has it that in the beginning, human beings prayed with their arms stretched wide open while God came and went among them. Then they built cathedrals with lofty spires and prayed with their hands pressed tightly to their chests. This chased God up into the heavens. But there is a rumor, the story concludes, that God is making the full circuit and that even now, he is coming up through the rich, dark loam of the earth.[1] The modern underworld journeys we have described can be thought of as part of the process of the rebirth of God. As I reflect on the modern versions of Inanna's, Demeter's, and Psyche's stories, it strikes me that God is indicated in all of them, precisely by the quest for a worthy object of devotion each of them imply. Plath's worship of her father, Woolf's nostalgia for her mother, Etty's ecstatic response to Spier—all these loves can be seen to point beyond themselves. If it is only Etty who moved explicitly from seeking God through the other to relating to God through herself, her journey nevertheless seems to reveal the truth of the others.

When Etty's journey is superimposed on Plath's, Plath's desire to die appears to anticipate the release Etty experiences when she lets go of Spier and says yes to death. The missing element in Plath, of course, is faith, which makes Etty's yes to death a trusting surrender of self rather than a despairing flight from self. Suicide and rebirth are very close; when one makes the underworld journey without faith, suicide, in one form or another, is inevitable. Alongside Plath, the stories of Joan Didion and Mary Gordon seem to portray women backpedaling away from the underworld journey: Charlotte's denial of the loss of her daughter and Felicitas's resolute refusal of romance after her tragic love affair appear to be attempts to protect the heart by closing it. But when we put their stories alongside Etty's, we can see that the two women's hearts are still open: Charlotte's love for Marin, even through a false image, is still love and Felicitas's attachment to her child is heartfelt. To quote Plath, "The heart does not stop."[2] Out of her pain, she expressed this truth despairingly. But it can also be an expression of hope. Despite ourselves, we go on loving, even when we have suffered from love. Against our better judgment, as it were, we stay open to life and, therefore, to the possibility of rebirth.

Rebirth occurs, it seems, when our desire for life and our desire to die—to be released from this life—come together. This is what happens when Etty says yes to the deep loneliness and lets go of Spier—the man to whom she was clinging with all the force of her residual desire for life. The deep loneliness in itself—"unrecognized," as we put it—can be seen as the desire to die: when it is dominant in the soul a person seeks, consciously or unconsciously, release from the life she knows and death is avoided by a constant struggle. But when the deep loneliness is met by the desire for life—when release from self is also and primarily gift of self—new life rises up in the soul. Etty's faith, it seems, was simply that her desire for life—even in the face of death—was not in vain, that she could let go of the life she was living, as death requires, and enter into a new life. The rebirth of God in our time would seem to come about when our primordial desire for life comes to term in that larger life that rises up in us when our yes to death is an act of love. Etty discovered the larger life, we can see, because she trusted that when her soul could no longer cling to Spier, it could cleave to God.

God as the life of my soul! What a distance we have come from the image of a remote and inaccessible sky god who dominates the consciousness of many women. After three years of writing this book, I am in touch with the "deeply buried woman" my poem of many years ago invoked. She emerges, I can see, when the heart of a woman is freed up from the cultural myth according to which woman finds her ful-fillment through a man and seeks its real fulfillment. The cultural myth locks her into the role of the pristine child of the fairy tales who equates good with light or the familiar and evil with darkness or the unknown. The hag-figure—her own anger—is frightening to the woman who identifies with the pristine child simply because it threatens the way of life she knows. But "killing the child," i.e., allowing one's rage to take over the personality, as we saw with Plath, is no solution. According to the myth, this represents the triumph of evil and can only be an act of despair. As Jung says, myths must be outgrown; attempting to defy their logic when we have no other meaning to live by can be disastrous. It is the pristine child, our study indicates, who leads us to the divine child. On one level, it is the fairy-tale truth that good always wins over evil that gives a woman who is lost—whose pristine child has been wounded by rejection—the courage to express her anguish to the unknown. And this is where the inward journey can become a journey with God.

As we saw, a woman might rest in the discovery of her divine child—in the knowledge that she and God are "con-nected," that there is a still point, a point of eternity in her—which provides the authentic foundation for all her acts of self-assertion. Finding the still point represents the healing of the divided self; it appears when I am willing to be the person that I am, when I am willing to be the crying child and I may simply desire to live out of that wholeness. Expressing myself and resting in myself—this is the alternation that may characterize my days. But in every encounter with God, a flame of love is enkindled in the soul. It is the divine passion of Psyche—the heart's response to mystery. As Etty saw, the lover's choice is to say yes to one's heart's desire and enter into a relationship with God. This is what she meant by "saying 'God'," calling the holy mystery by name. Even Etty, who had no dark images of God to exorcise from her soul was in wonderment at the depth and intimacy of this relationship. When I consent to be led by my heart's desire, I am letting God be the life of my self, we could say; when I consent to be led by my heart's desire through death, God becomes the life of my soul.

Where am I standing when God is the life of my self and soul? In Christian terms, I am standing in the place of Jesus, the incarnate Word of God, and the life I experience is my participation in the life of the Trinity. The Gospel of Matthew that Etty was reading "morning and night" does not portray Jesus as the Word made flesh and it is likely that Etty did not think of her standpoint in these terms. Yet a Christian cannot help but see Etty as a Christ-figure, i.e., as someone who herself gives witness to the divine love that we see in Jesus. For me, Etty is the link between the goddess tradition and Christianity; she demonstrates that there is what we might call a goddess trajectory to Christianity. Is this so surprising? St. Augustine (whom Etty was fond of reading) was one Christian theologian who did not think so. He seems to be saying that knowledge of the *Logos*, of the Word of God, can be found among people who never even heard of Christ when he writes, "The ancients also knew what is now called the Christian religion and this existed from the very beginning until Christ appeared in the flesh."[3] The presence of the *Logos* at the heart of creation responds to our essential desire, which is for an intimate relationship with the living God. The wisdom of the goddess tradition, to which Etty was faithful, is to honor our deepest feelings and desires, trusting that they will lead us to a reality greater than the self.

Yet trusting our desires is only the beginning of the journeys we have described. We must also trust the darkness into which we are plunged when we come up against loss—when all that we know is the unfulfillment of our desires. When a woman's pristine child cries out her pain, she is ultimately relying in the "deeply buried woman" in herself. As much as the child fears the darkness, the deeply buried woman knows to open herself to it. And it is from the embrace of the deeply buried woman and the darkness that the divine child is born: it is only our intuition of the presence of God in the darkness—an intuition that breaks, once and for all, our restriction of God to the light—that enables us to wait in the darkness; from this waiting comes knowledge that we are known by God. How many women have never trusted the darkness! Rigidly identified with their pristine child, they are ashamed to be unhappy. Their experiences of pain and loss are never fruitful. In my experience, religion that worships God as an exalted judge, as important as it is for affirming the triumph of good over evil, cannot by itself free a woman from the stranglehold of her pristine child. The goddess tradition is essential, I would say, for a woman like me to experience wholeness in relation to God.

Without wholeness and relying on one's wholeness, the next stage of the journey—relying on heart's desire—is not possible. Without wholeness, all I can rely on is the life-force—the desire to live truncated in me, I now see, by my fear of death. Heart's desire first emerges as other than the life-force. It first appeared in Etty as the desire for the mysterious life that she saw in Spier—a desire that pointed her in the opposite direction from her instinctual tendency to possess him. But the desire only became effectual, we saw, as she opened herself to the darkness—first to the darkness at the center of herself, then to the darkness of suffering, and finally, to the darkness of death. Unless it is the whole woman who meets the darkness, darkness only reinforces my reliance on the life-force. But when my confrontation with the darkness becomes a waiting in the dark, my fear of the dark can be overcome and this effects a release of my heart's desire. As I wait in the dark-ness at the center of myself, I come to an awareness of God and this releases heart's desire as the desire for the journey with God. As I wait in the darkness of suffering, I come to an aware-ness of the love that encompasses and sustains me in the midst of my suffering. This releases my whole heart for the journey. As I wait in the darkness for death, I come to an awareness of the larger life—eternal life, in theological terms—in which God and I are one. This releases my soul for the journey.

In the experience of the larger life, there is no opposi-tion between my desire for God, for the journey with God, and my desire for life. The conflagration in the soul that Etty remarks upon signals a love that consumes the whole person. This, it seems, is the ultimate resolution of the split I ex-pressed in my poem. The wholeness of the "deeply buried woman" in herself is something holy, based as it is on her ac-ceptance of herself as known by God. But the heart wants more. The story of Demeter and Persephone is completed by the story of Psyche. The whole woman wants to be wholly in love with God. When Etty pauses in her headlong pursuit of her heart's desire, she sometimes expresses dismay at the distance she has traveled from her old, familiar life. Her con-tinual references to her native dream of devoting herself to a man can be seen as attempts to compensate for her increasing spiritual independence. At first blush, there is something dreadful in the vision of a life which is not determined by the need for human ties. We can imagine a woman, afraid of where her heart is leading, praying for a "normal life," for a husband and children. She may get her normal life, but she will only get what she really wants when she goes with the folly of her heart's desire. Etty's genius, it seems to me, and this reflects her alignment with the goddess tradition, is that she recognizes the folly of her heart's desire as a higher wisdom.

Against the influence of a remote sky god in a woman's life, the figures of Inanna, Demeter, and Psyche encourage her to trust her heart. The rage of the hag-queen, in Inanna's story, we see now is a blind expression of heart's desire. A woman rages in the face of loss and death because she thinks that what she wants is power—the power of life against death. In this case, heart's desire is undifferentiated from the life-force. Differentiation occurs when a woman gives birth to her divine child—when, in the knowledge of herself as known by God she finds a place to stand beyond the struggle of life against death. Where I know myself as known by God is spirit; the gentle heart of Demeter emerging from her temple reflects a knowledge of the deeper life of spirit. To remain at the standpoint of Demeter is to enjoy the peacefulness of the deeper life. But the heart, at this standpoint, is not wholly peaceful. The part of the heart that feels with the body is still caught in the struggle of life against death. The gentle heart of Demeter becomes the passionate heart of Psyche in the fire that is enkindled when I let go of the object of my passion and say yes to the deep loneliness. The sky god, it seems, has become aligned with the cold gods, with death. The fire in the soul that frees me from the fear of death frees me, once and for all, from my worship of the sky god.

The rebirth of God occurs, then, when human beings themselves are reborn. There is an image from the goddess tradition which captures the beauty and power of the emergence of the "deeply buried woman." Lucius Apuleius, an initiate into the mysteries of the great goddess Isis, completes his ritual of rebirth by dipping himself seven times in the sea under a full moon. After the last immersion, while he is praying to the goddess with tears streaming down his face, he has a vision. A woman with a beautiful face and shining body rises up from the middle of the sea. There is a halo above her brow, a moon and stars on her black mantle, and two serpents rising up from the thick ringlets of her hair.[4] What a contrast this presents from the image of my childhood of a pristine virgin crushing the serpent's head! How the religion of a sky god has separated women from their native endowment—the enormous energy of the desire for life. The goddess trajectory to Christianity demonstrates that our desire for life is not destroyed by a relationship with God, but rather, that a relationship with the living God encompasses it. There is discontinuity between my primordial desire for life and the fire of love in my soul that is eternal life, but there is also continuity.

A priest friend once told me about a conversation he had with a young woman who wanted to marry him. He told her that he was not free to marry because he had consecrated himself to God. "Turn to life," was the woman's reply, "God is in your heart." A woman's native inclination is to turn to life. This does not change once she has fulfilled the purpose of the underworld journey and made the discovery of eternal life. She is ready to plunge once more into work and relationships. But she engages in work with others now from a new foundation—a soul in love with God. So her desire for life is no longer desperate. She enjoys her old ecstasies but she does not cling to them. If her soul should require that she give them up altogether, it is all the same to her. This is freedom for a woman—to be in the midst of the things of life without being determined by an experience of the life-force that is craven because of her fear of death. Reentering life relying on your soul surely marks the beginning of another journey. In the last pages of her diary, thinking back over the growth she has experienced in the previous one and a half years, Etty nevertheless declares, "my real work has not begun."[5] But it is the work that will be carried out, we know, in the joy that is the fruit of the underworld journey.

Notes

PREFACE

1. See, for example, *Freeing Theology: The Essentials of Theology in Feminist Perspective,* ed. Catherine Mowry LaCugna (San Francisco: Harper, 1993).

2. Virginia Woolf, *Night and Day* (New York: Harcourt Brace Jovanovich, 1974), 484.

3. Carol Lee Flinders, *At the Root of This Longing, Reconciling a Spiritual Hunger with a Feminist Thirst* (San Francisco: Harper, 1998).

ONE: THE ALTERNATIVE TRADITION

1. St. Augustine, Tractates on the first letter of John, Tractate 1.3: PL 35, 1978, 1980, as quoted in *The Liturgy of the Hours* (Daughters of St. Paul, St. Paul Editions, 1976), 1652.

2. St. Bonaventure, *The Mind's Road to God,* trans. George Boas (Indianapolis and New York: Library of Liberal Arts, Bobbs-Merrill, 1953).

3. Ibid., 4.

4. Ibid.

5. Fyodor Dostoyevsky, *The Idiot,* trans. Constance Garnett (New York: Modern Library, Random House, 1935), 10.

6. Evelyn Waugh, *Brideshead Revisited* (Boston: Little, Brown, 1945), 221.

7. Catherine of Siena, quoted in Elizabeth Alvide Petroff, *Body and Soul: Essays on Medieval Women and Mysticism* (New York and Oxford: Oxford University Press, 1994), 4.

8. Waugh, *Brideshead Revisited*, 31.

9. Ibid., 351.

10. Ibid., 350.

11. Diane Wolkstein and Samuel Noah Kramer, "The Descent of Inanna," in *Inanna, Queen of Heaven and Earth* (New York: Harper and Row, 1983), 51–73.

12. N. K. Sanders, *The Epic of Gilgamesh* (New York: Penguin Books, 1972), 83.

13. Wolkstein and Kramer, "Descent of Inanna," 29–50.

14. Apostolos N. Athanassakis, *To Demeter* in *The Homeric Hymns* (Baltimore and London: Johns Hopkins University Press, 1976).

15. Erich Neumann, *Amor and Psyche: The Psychic Development of the Feminine*, trans. Ralph Manheim (New York: Bollingen Foundation, Princeton University Press, 1956).

16. Marija Gimbutas, *The Civilization of the Goddess: The World of Old Europe* (New York: Harper Collins, 1991).

17. Ibid.

18. Charlene Spretnak, *Lost Goddesses of Early Greece: A Collection of Pre-Hellenic Myths* (Boston: Beacon Press, 1978).

19. Ibid., 35.

20. Ibid., 22–23.

21. Carol Christ, *Laughter of Aphrodite: Reflections on a Journey to the Goddess* (San Francisco: Harper and Row, 1983), 5.

22. Wolkstein and Kramer, "Descent of Inanna," 5.

23. Ibid., 12.

24. Sanders, *Epic of Gilgamesh*, 85–87.

25. See, for example, Riane Eisler, *The Chalice and the Blade* (San Francisco: Harper and Row, 1987), and Merlin Stone, *When God Was a Woman* (New York and London: Harcourt Brace Jovanovich, 1976) as well as the books by Charlene Spretnak and Carol Christ, already cited.

26. Gimbutas, *Civilization of the Goddess*, 238.

27. William Vaughan Moody, "The Death of Eve," in *The Poems and Plays of William Vaughan Moody*, vol. 1 (Boston and New York: Houghton Mifflin, 1912), 436.

28. Sylvia Plath, *Collected Poems*, ed. Ted Hughes (New York: Harper and Row, 1981), 223.

29. See, for example, The Book of Amos, *New American Bible* (Nashville and New York: Thomas Nelson, 1971), 1017–1025.

30. Susan Griffin, "This Earth Is My Sister" in *Weaving the Visions*, ed. Judith Plaskow and Carol Christ (San Francisco: Harper and Row, 1989), 110.

31. Wolkstein and Kramer, "Descent of Inanna," 40.

32. Kierkegaard actually says, "with God, everything is possible," in *The Sickness unto Death*, trans. Howard V. and Edna Hong (Princeton, N.J.: Princeton University Press, 1980), 38.

33. See, for example, Jeremiah 2:1–6.

TWO: INANNA, DEMETER, AND PSYCHE

1. Wolkstein and Kramer, "Descent of Inanna," 51–73.

2. Ibid., 55.

3. Ibid., 56–57.

4. Ibid., 60.

5. Ibid.

6. Ibid., 68.

7. Ibid., 71.

8. Ibid.

9. Beverly Wildung Harrison, "The Power of Anger in the Work of Love," in *Weaving the Visions*, ed. Judith Plaskow and Carol Christ (San Francisco: Harper and Row, 1989), 217.

10. See, for example, Simone Weil, *Waiting for God*, trans. Emma Crawford (New York: Harper and Row, 1973), 202.

11. Kierkegaard, *Sickness unto Death*, 77.

12. Athanasskis, *To Demeter*.

13. James Joyce, *Finnegans Wake* (New York: Viking Press, Compass Books Edition, 1959), 627.

14. Simone Weil to Albertine Thevenon in *Seventy Letters*, trans. Richard Rees (London: Oxford University Press, 1962), 19.

15. Weil, *Waiting for God*, 131.

16. Neumann, *Amor and Psyche*. I am using the Greek name for the god of love, Eros, rather than the Roman appellation, Amor.

17. Ibid., 5.

18. Ibid., 6.

19. Ibid., 18.

20. Ibid., 40.

21. Ibid., 44.

22. Ibid., 50.

23. Ibid., 52.

24. Ibid., 53.

25. Marcel Proust, Á la recherché du temps perdu, vol. 1 (Paris: Gallimerol, Bibliotheque de la Pleiede, 1954), 100, as quoted in John S. Dunne, The Reasons of the Heart (Notre Dame, Ind.: University of Notre Dame Press, 1978), Dunne's translation.

26. D. H. Lawrence, "The Man Who Died," in The Later D. H. Lawrence (New York: Alfred A. Knopf, 1952), 426–427.

27. Neumann, Amor and Psyche, 57 161.

28. Ibid., 25.

29. I get this expression from a lecture given by John S. Dunne in a course he taught at the University of Notre Dame in the 1970s.

30. Neumann, Amor and Psyche, 29.

31. Thomas Merton, Conjectures of a Guilty Bystander (New York: Image Books, Doubleday, 1968), 157.

32. Ibid., 158.

33. Weil, Waiting for God, 105–116.

34. Ibid.

35. Ibid., 166.

36. C. S. Lewis, The Lion, the Witch, and the Wardrobe (New York: Collier Books, Macmillan, 1970), 138–139.

37. Neumann, Amor and Psyche, 112.

38. Unpublished poem of mine in a collection entitled "Death Poems."

39. Simone Weil, Gravity and Grace, trans. Arthur Wills (New York: Octagon Books, Farrar, Straus, and Giroux, 1979), 134.

40. Lewis, The Lion, the Witch, and the Wardrobe, 159.

41. Joyce, Finnegans Wake, 212–216.

THREE: THE CHILD AND THE HAG: SYLVIA PLATH

1. James Joyce, Portrait of the Artist as a Young Man (New York: Viking Press, 1964), 252.

2. Ibid., 252–253.

3. Robert Graves, *The White Goddess* (New York: Noonday Press, 1948), 35.

4. Gimbutas, *Civilization of the Goddess*, 399.

5. Kate Chopin, *The Awakening and Other Stories*, ed. Lewis Leary (New York: Holt, Rinehart, and Winston, 1970), 199–341.

6. Margaret Atwood, *Surfacing* (New York: Warner Books, 1972).

7. Sylvia Plath, *The Bell Jar* (New York: Harper and Row, 1971).

8. Plath, *Collected Poems*, 31.

9. Nancy Hunter Steiner, *A Closer Look at Ariel* (New York: Harper's Magazine Press, 1973), 42.

10. Judith Kroll, *Chapters in a Mythology* (New York: Harper and Row, 1976), 39–43.

11. Ibid., 220 (note 19).

12. Ibid., 116.

13. Plath, *Collected Poems*, 32.

14. Ibid., 29–30.

15. William Broyles, "Why Men Love War," in *Making War/ Making Peace*, ed. Francesca Cancian and James William Gibson (Belmont, Calif: Wadsworth, 1990), 35.

16. Plath, *Collected Poems*, 54–56.

17. For a discussion of the alternation of the powers of sexuality and death in the myths involving Inanna and Dumuzi of ancient Sumer, see Wolkstein and Kramer, *Inanna, Queen of Heaven and Earth*, 165–169.

18. Plath, *Collected Poems*, 69–70.

19. Sylvia Plath, *Letters Home*, ed. Aurelia Plath (New York: Harper and Row, 1975), 25.

20. Plath, *Collected Poems*.

21. Plath, *The Bell Jar*, 188–189.

22. Ibid., 267.

23. Ibid., 274.

24. Ibid., 275.

25. Ibid.

26. Ibid., 267.

27. Plath, *Collected Poems*, 92–93.

28. Ibid., 74–76.

29. Ibid., 24–25.

30. Ibid., 94–95.

31. Ibid., 92–93.

32. Anne Sexton, "The Barfly Ought to Sing" in *Ariel Ascending*, ed. Paul Alexander (New York: Harper and Row, 1985), 179.

33. Ibid., 180.

34. Doris Lessing, "To Room Nineteen," in *Stories* (New York: Random House, Vintage Books, 1980), 428.

35. Plath, *Letters Home*, 277.

36. Plath, *Collected Poems*, 149–150.

37. Ibid., 158–159.

38. George Stade, "Introduction" to Nancy Hunter Steiner, *A Closer Look at Ariel* (New York: Harpers Magazine Press, 1973), 5.

39. Plath, *Collected Poems*, 160–162.

40. Judith Kroll, "The Central Symbolism of the Moon," in *Chapters in a Mythology*, 21–79.

41. Plath, *Collected Poems*, 171–173.

42. Kroll, *Chapters in a Mythology* 21–79.

43. Sylvia Plath, *The Journals of Sylvia Plath*, ed. Ted Hughes and Frances McCullough (New York: Dial Press, 1982), 272.

44. Plath, *Collected Poems*, 176–187.

45. Ibid., 192–193.

46. Michael Mott, *Seven Mountains of Thomas Merton* (Boston: Houghton Mifflin, 1984), 448–449.

47. Plath, *Collected Poems*, "Apprehensions," 195–196.

48. Ibid., "The Rabbit Catcher," 193–194.

49. Ibid., 201–202.

50. Ibid., 214–315.

51. Simone Weil, *The Iliad, Poem of Force* (Wallingford, Penn.: Pendle Hill, 1956), 14.

52. Quoted in Ted Hughes, "Sylvia Plath and Her Journals," in *Ariel Ascending* (New York: Harper and Row, 1985), 163.

53. Sexton, "The Barfly Ought to Sing," 179.

54. A. Alvarez, "Sylvia Plath: A Memoir," *New American Review*, no. 12 (New York: Simon and Schuster, Touchstone Books, 1971), 9–40; quoted in Kroll, *Chapters in a Mythology*, 261.

55. Ted Hughes, "Foreword" to *The Journals of Sylvia Plath*, xii.

56. Plath, *Collected Poems*, 206–208.

57. Ibid., 208–209.

58. Ibid., 147.

59. Ibid., 214.

60. This is a phrase from an unpublished poem of mine entitled "The Long March."

61. Plath, *Collected Poems*, 215.

62. Chopin, *The Awakening and Other Stories*, 301.

63. Plath, *Collected Poems*, 265.

64. Ibid., 332–324.

65. Sylvia Plath quoted by George Stade, "Introduction" to Steiner, *A Closer Look at Ariel*, 12.

66. Plath, *Collected Poems*, 224–226.

67. Plath, *Letters Home*, 465.

68. Atwood, *Surfacing*, 49.

69. Plath, *Collected Poems*, "Years," 255–256.

70. Ibid., "Ariel," 239–240.

71. Leo Tolstoy, quoted in Wolkstein and Kramer, *Inanna, Queen of Heaven and Earth*, 156.

72. Plath, *Collected Poems*, 244–246.

73. Ibid., 242–244.

74. Ibid., 254–255.

75. Ibid., 208.

76. Ibid., 247–249.

77. Walker Percy, *The Second Coming* (New York: Ballantine Books, 1980), 66.

78. Plath, *Collected Poems*, "Mary's Song," 257.

79. According to Judith Kroll, Ted Hughes remarked in conversation that several times during the last two or three weeks of her life she said something to the effect that "I have seen God, and he keeps picking me up" and "I am full of God" (Kroll, *Chapters in a Mythology*, 177).

80. Plath, *Collected Poems*, 268– 269.

81. Ibid.

82. Plath, *Collected Poems*, 269.

83. Ibid., 227–230.

84. Ibid., 262.

85. Ibid., 264–265.

86. Ibid., 270.

87. Ibid., "Kindness," 269–270.

88. Ibid., "Child," 265.

89. Ibid., "Edge," 272–273.

FOUR: THE CHILD AND THE MOTHER:
JOAN DIDION, MARY GORDON, VIRGINIA WOOLF

1. Simone Weil, *Two Moral Essays* (Wallingford, Penn.: Pendle Hill, Pamphlet #240, 1981), 14.

2. Plath, *Collected Poems*, "Mystic," 269.

3. Liv Ullmann, *Changing* (London: Weidenfeld and Nicolson, 1977).

4. Joan Didion, *A Book of Common Prayer* (New York: Pocket Books, 1977), 42.

5. Ibid., 4.

6. Ibid., 14.

7. Ibid., 110–111.

8. Ibid., 14.

9. Ibid., 124.

10. Ibid., 6.

11. Ibid., 13.

12. Ibid., 5.

13. Ibid., 120.

14. Ibid., 280.

15. Ibid., 276.

16. Plath, *Journals of Sylvia Plath*, 213.

17. Didion, *Book of Common Prayer*, 3.

18. Ibid., 4.

19. Ibid.

20. Ibid., 280.

21. Mary Gordon, *The Company of Women* (New York: Random House, 1980), 254.

22. Waugh, *Brideshead Revisited*, 169.

23. Weil, *Two Moral Essays*, 10.

24. Gordon, *The Company of Women*, 46.

25. Ibid., 288.

26. Ibid., 277.

27. Ibid., 278.

28. Ibid., 277.

29. Ibid., 280.

30. Ibid., 282–283.

31. William Butler Yeats, "For Anne Gregory," in *The Collected Poems* (New York: Macmillan, 1956), 240.

32. Gordon, *The Company of Women*, 243–244.

33. Ibid., 273.

34. Ibid., 284.

35. Ibid., 287.

36. Ibid., 284.

37. Ibid., 244.

38. Ibid., 252.

39. Ibid., 261.

40. Ibid., 265.

41. Ibid.

42. Ibid., 264.

43. Gimbutas, *Civilization of the Goddess*, 399.

44. Gordon, *The Company of Women*, 260.

45. Ibid., 243.

46. Ibid., 291.

47. Ibid., 284.

48. Ibid., 253.

49. Ibid.

50. Ibid., 263.

51. Ibid., 260.

52. Ibid., 264.

53. Ibid.

54. Ibid., 265.

55. See Chapter 2, note 29.

56. Sylvia Plath in *A Closer Look at Ariel*, 12.

57. Quentin Bell, *Virginia Woolf* (New York: Harcourt Brace Jovanovich, 1972) vol. 1, 40.

58. Woolf, *Night and Day*, 484.

59. Ibid., 485.

60. Ibid., 483.

61. Ibid., 493.

62. Bell, *Virginia Woolf*, vol. 2, 226.

63. Virginia Woolf, *To the Lighthouse* (New York: Harcourt Brace Jovanovich, 1989), 41.

64. Ibid., 51.

65. Ibid., 50.

66. Ibid., 62–63.

67. Ibid., 97.

68. Ibid., 161.

69. Ibid., 134.

70. Ibid., 19.

71. Ibid.

72. Etty Hillesum, *An Interrupted Life: The Diaries of Etty Hillesum* (New York: Washington Square Press, 1981), 51.

73. Woolf, *To the Lighthouse*, 157.

74. Bell, *Virginia Woolf*, vol. 2, 100.

75. Virginia Woolf, *Mrs. Dalloway* (New York: Harcourt, Brace, and World, 1953), 220.

76. Woolf, *To the Lighthouse*, 159.

77. Ibid., 160.

78. Ibid., 171.

79. Ibid., 161.

80. Bell, *Virginia Woolf*, vol. 2, 89.

81. Ibid.

82. Woolf, *To the Lighthouse*, 178.

83. Ibid.

84. C. G. Jung and C. Kerenyi, *Essays on a Science of Mythology*, trans. R. F. C. Hull (Princeton, N.J.: Princeton University Press, 1949), 143.

85. Woolf, *To the Lighthouse*, 180.

86. Bell, *Virginia Woolf*, vol. 2, 118.

87. Woolf, *To the Lighthouse*, 181.

88. Ibid., 209.

89. Thomas Merton, *New Seeds of Contemplation* (New York: Directions Books, 1962), 297.

FIVE: THE WOMAN AND GOD: ETTY HILLESUM

1. Plath, *Collected Poems*, 268.

2. I get this expression from lectures given by John Dunne in courses he taught at the University of Notre Dame in the 1970s.

3. Hillesum, An Interrupted Life, 3.

4. Ibid., 1–2.

5. Ibid., 2.

6. Ibid., 20.

7. Ibid., 7.

8. Ibid., 14.

9. Joyce, *Finnegans Wake*, 627.

10. This ruthlessness towards her emotions is especially to be found in one of her early notebooks, quoted in Simone Petrement, *Simone Weil: A Life,* trans. Raymond Rosenthal (New York: Pantheon Books, 1976), 220.

11. Hillesum, *An Interrupted Life,* 5.

12. Ibid., 25.

13. Ibid., 40.

14. Ibid., 26.

15. Ibid.

16. Ibid.

17. Ibid., 34.

18. Ibid., 27–28.

19. Ibid., 38.

20. Ibid., 51.

21. Ibid., 26.

22. Ibid., 67.

23. Ibid., 18.

24. Ibid., 65.

25. Ibid., 56.

26. Ibid.

27. Ibid., 26.

28. Ibid., 27.

29. Ibid., 57.

30. Ibid., 49–50.

31. Ibid., 55.

32. Ibid.

33. Ibid., 44.

34. Ibid., 62.

35. Ibid.

36. Albert Camus, quoted in John Dunne, *The Reasons of the Heart* (Notre Dame, Ind.: University of Notre Dame Press, 1978), 18.

37. Simone Weil, *The Notebooks of Simone Weil,* trans. Arthur F. Wills (New York: Putnam's Sons, 1956), vol. 1, 30.

38. Hillesum, *An Interrupted Life,* 64–65.

39. Ibid., 65.

40. Ibid., 81.

41. Ntozake Shange, quoted in Carol Christ, *Diving Deep and Surfing* (Boston: Beacon Press, 1980), 97.

42. This was the main theme of a lecture Alice Walker delivered in Burlington, Vermont, in November 1996.

43. Hillesum, *An Interrupted Life*, 76.

44. Ibid., 85.

45. Ibid., 76.

46. About an experience she had while visiting a chapel in Assisi, Weil writes, "something stronger than I compelled me for the first time in my life to go down on my knees" in *Waiting for God*, 67–68.

47. Hillesum, *An Interrupted Life*, 76.

48. Weil, *Seventy Letters*, 91.

49. Weil, *Gravity and Grace*, 108.

50. Susan Griffin, quoted in Sherry Roth Anderson and Patricia Hopkins, *The Feminine Face of God* (New York: Bantam Books, 1991), 190.

51. Hillesum, *An Interrupted Life*, 72.

52. Wendell Berry, *A World Lost* (Washington, D.C.: Counterpoint, 1996), 149.

53. Hillesum, *An Interrupted Life*, 75.

54. Ibid., 75–76.

55. Ibid., 91.

56. Ibid., 59.

57. Ibid., 90.

58. Ibid.

59. Ibid., 105.

60. Ibid., 95.

61. Ibid., 108.

62. Ibid., 112.

63. Ibid.

64. Ibid., 100.

65. Quoted in Cal Thomas, "China's House Churches Flourish," *Burlington Free Press*, July 7, 1997, p. 6A.

66. Hillesum, *An Interrupted Life*, 11.

67. Ibid., 10.

68. Ibid., 100–101.

69. Quoted in Anderson and Hopkins, *The Feminine Face of God*, 63.

70. Ibid.

71. Weil, *Gravity and Grace*, 55.

72. Hillesum, *An Interrupted Life*, 99.

73. Ibid., 147.

74. Lewis, *The Lion, the Witch, and the Wardrobe*, 138–139.

75. Hillesum, *An Interrupted Life*, 99.

76. Ibid., 151.

77. Ibid., 160.

78. Ibid., 105–106.

79. Ibid., 96.

80. Ibid., 141.

81. Audre Lorde, "The Use of the Erotic," in *Weaving the Visions*, ed. Judith Plaskow and Carol Christ (San Francisco: Harper and Row, 1989), 213.

82. Ibid., 209.

83. Hillesum, *An Interrupted Life*, 108.

84. Ibid., 132.

85. Ibid., 103.

86. Ibid., 186.

87. Ibid., 159.

88. Ibid., 157.

89. Ibid.

90. Dunne, *Reasons of the Heart*, 3 and *passim*.

91. Hillesum, *An Interrupted Life*, 96.

92. Herbert Mason, *The Death of Al-Hallaj* (Notre Dame, Ind.: University of Notre Dame Press, 1979), 17.

93. Hillesum, *An Interrupted Life*, 128.

94. Ibid., 131.

95. Ibid., 169.

96. Ibid., 160.

97. D. H. Lawrence, "The Man Who Died," in *The Later D. H. Lawrence*, 414.

98. Hillesum, *An Interrupted Life*, 171–172.

99. Ibid., 172.

100. Ibid., 188.

101. Ibid., 193.

102. Ibid., 209–210.

103. Ibid., 211.

104. Ibid., 212.

105. Quoted in *Roses in December*, a film by Ana Carrigan.

106. Matthew 22:32.

107. Hillesum, *An Interrupted Life*, 213.

108. Ibid., 215.

109. Ibid., 219.

110. Ibid., 239.

111. Ibid., 113.

112. Ibid., 222–223.

113. Ibid., 234.

114. Ibid., 243.

115. John 10:10.

116. Daniel Berrigan, "Foreword" to Philip Berrigan and Elizabeth McAlister, *The Times Discipline* (Baltimore: Fortkamp, 1989), xvi.

117. Hillesum, *An Interrupted Life*, 241.

SIX: THE GODDESS TRAJECTORY TO CHRISTIANITY

1. Maria Rainer Rilke, *Stories of God* (New York: W. W. Norton, 1963), 87–89.

2. Plath, *Collected Poems*, 269.

3. Augustine, quoted in *The Soul Afire* (New York: Pantheon Books, 1944), 3.

4. Anne Baring and Jules Cashford, *The Myth of the Goddess* (London: Viking Books, 1991), 272.

5. Hillesum, *An Interrupted Life*, 227.

Index

action, appeal of, 34, 47
aloneness, 81–85, 89; of death,
    82–83, 86, 125; denial of,
    139; fear of, 133, 135; in
    Plath, 81–82, 87, 89–90; rage
    and grief over, 99; and the
    void, 87, 155–58. *See also*
    loneliness
anger: over aloneness, 99; against
    death, 52, 72, 86, 89, 170;
    of Demeter, 36–37; God-
    the-Father tradition and,
    29–30; in Hillesum, 170;
    in "Inanna's Descent," 23–30,
    39, 52, 197; over loss of
    love, 90; of Plath, 74, 78, 80,
    84–87, 89–90, 94, 193; and
    powerlessness, 25, 30, 82;
    as reaction to suffering, 171;
    spiritual journeys as antidote
    to, 170. *See also* hag-queen,
    the
anxiety, 32, 39, 46
Aphrodite, 50
Apuleius, Lucius, 197
art, 87, 132–37

attachments: to another, 54, 85, 88,
    135, 167, 183–84; to the
    ideal, 106, 116
"attention," enkindling the divine
    spark through, 51
Atwood, Margaret: *Surfacing*, 66,
    91
Augustine, Saint, 1, 194

beauty: and God-the-Father
    tradition, 20–21; and image
    of someone desired, xii, 1;
    of mediating figures, 49; of
    nature, 16, 20–21, 175, 177;
    sacramental nature of, 57
Berrigan, Daniel, 190
Berry, Wendell, 164–65
Bonaventure, Saint, 2, 4
breakthrough experiences, 15–16,
    46, 159. *See also* heart's
    release
Broyles, William, 69

Camus, Albert, 160; "The
    Adulterous Wife," 143, 182
care, having a, 33, 38, 119–20